INTRODUCTION TO
BUSINESS

DANTES/DSST* Study Guide

© 2011 Breely, Crush & Associates, LLC

*DSST is a registered trademark of The Thomson Corporation and its affiliated companies, and does not endorse this book.

97162411143

Published by Breely Crush Publishing
10808 River Front Parkway
South Jordan, UT 84095
www.breelycrushpublishing.com

ISBN-10: 1-61433-050-6
ISBN-13: 978-1-61433-050-9

Printed and bound in the United States of America.

*DSST is a registered trademark of The Thomson Corporation and its affiliated companies, and does not endorse this book.

Table of Contents

Economic Issues

Economics is the study of how people choose to use limited resources to satisfy people's unlimited wants. Social responsibility is the idea that a business is part of something bigger than itself. It is part of a global community. With that knowledge comes the responsibility to do what is best for the company and for society as well. Some of the ways that companies can contribute to society are making environmentally friendly choices as well as contributing to charities.

There are four factors of production:

1. labor – the human resource, brain and brawn
2. land – includes all natural resources
3. capital – funds provided by investors and profits created
4. entrepreneurship – the processes of bringing the other factors together to create a good or service and a profit

Socialism is an economic system. Unlike capitalism, the government does the economic planning, owns most of the basic industries, controls the large industries and has a heavy tax to finance the welfare programs of the nation. Typical industries owned by a socialist government include coal mining, banking, major transportation like air, rail, etc. Some current social democracies include: Great Britain, Italy, Sweden, France and Austria. Under this system, the country supplies medical care, dental care, and college education.

Theory and Practice of Management

WHAT IS MANAGING ALL ABOUT?

In a broader sense, Management may be defined as working with people and groups of people with the sole intention of achieving organizational goals. From this definition you can see that the word "Management" is not tied down to managing business or industrial organizations. It has been given a broader perspective; Business, industry, educational institutions, political establishments, hospitals and nursing homes, churches and even families – come under its purview. People who manage should have interpersonal skills. Messrs. Paul Hersey and Kenneth Blanchard believe that "…the achievement of organizational objectives through leadership is Management…"

MANAGING – IS IT AN ART OR SCIENCE?

Managing is something which managers practice. They interact with people in an organization with a view to achieve organizational objectives. A Doctor practices medicine and an Accountant practices accountancy. They practice in their chosen fields because they have acquired skills. So, if we view managing as a practice, then it can be considered as an art. A science, however, needs systematic knowledge, crystal clear concepts, rational theories supported by experimentation and analysis. So, if we view management as a body of systematic knowledge, it can be considered as a science.

MANAGEMENT THEORIES

Management theories abound. In some way each theory has contributed a mite to the knowledge of management.

Theory	Its import in a nutshell
1. The Empirical or Case Approach	The experience of past situations to guide in the present. Find out why a particular action succeeded or failed by going deeper to analyze the basic reasons.
2. The Inter-personal behavior Approach	It is all about understanding people and their relationships. It mainly deals with the human aspect and stresses that if people understood other people perfectly, organizational goals could be achieved without much difficulty.
3. The Group-behavior Approach	In an organization people work not in isolation but in groups. The study of group behavior patterns is to know how groups affect production possibilities positively or negatively. It relates to the study of behavioral composition of groups, which are large, and how this impacts their relationships.
4. The Co-operative Social Systems Approach	As a corollary of the group behavior approach, the Co-operative Social System came into being. It deals with human relationship as a co-operative social system. Propounded by Christian Barnard, the essence of the co-operative social system is the co-operative interaction of thoughts, ideas, wants and desires of two or more people. His theory focuses on both interpersonal and group behavioral approaches and concludes that their interaction leads to a system of co-operation.

5. Socio-technical Systems Approach	Arising out of the co-operative social systems, another approach, mostly credited to E. L. Trist, seeks to emphasize the systems aspect of group behavior. It tries to relate group behavior with technical systems and those relationships. There should be a most harmonious relationship between groups of people (social systems) on the one hand and machines, systems and methods (technical system), on the other. It seeks to establish that personal behavior and group behavior are necessarily influenced by the technical system in which they work.
6. The Decision Theory Approach	This approach emphasizes that a Manager's most important function is Decision Making and therefore the decision should be the central focus. A manager goes ahead on the basis of evaluating innumerable alternatives and arriving at a most suitable decision, depending upon the facts and figures, and importantly, the extent to which he was delegated responsibility and authority. Since decision-making is the core, all the other functions of a manager are built around it, so say the decision theorists.
7. The Systems Approach	They view management as a system, which envelops within itself many subsystems, all operating within the total environment. A total unity, which is a collection interdependent of or interconnected with sub-systems working within a total environment. Concepts, ideas, thoughts, principles, theories or techniques (sub-system) in the area of managing (system).
8. The Mathematical or Management Science Approach	The Mathematical models form part of this theory. Each situation is considered in terms of available Mathematical models and then the situation is analyzed, arriving at a mathematically correct decision.

9. The Contingency or Situational Approach Professor. J. Lorsch of Harvard University was one of the founders of this theory.	It tells us that any manager's performance is directly related to a set of given circumstances or contingencies. Some theorists also feel that it takes into account not only situations but also the behavior pattern of an organization. The drawback is that instead of promoting total organizational loyalty, it encourages departmental loyalty.
10. The Managerial Roles Approach	This is the latest approach propounded by Professor Henry Mintzberg, to observe what managers do and using such observations as a platform for analyzing and concluding on the basis of such analysis, what their roles (i.e., activities) are. This approach has visibility. The Professor studied the roles of many Chief Executives and concluded that they not only perform the classical function of a Manager, such as planning, organizing, coordinating, leading and controlling, but also perform a variety of other functions as well.
11. The Operational Approach	This approach believes in imparting knowledge from every other field of knowledge such as sociology, Mathematics, Economics, Psychology, etc., which fits simply into Management

The Impact of External Environment

Every organization has to operate under different external environments. It is within the environment and therefore has to be responsive.

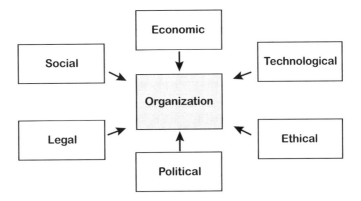

The operations of any organization whether domestic or international depend largely on these externals, which act as a constraining influence. In an international organization the impact of external influences is even more rigorous. A person deputed from a parent country to a host country has to be knowledgeable about the host country's economical, political, legal, educational, social and cultural environment.

Additionally, the management of an international company has to spend a lot of time in determining the orientation of management best suited to the host country. A birds-eye view of Management Orientation is represented by:

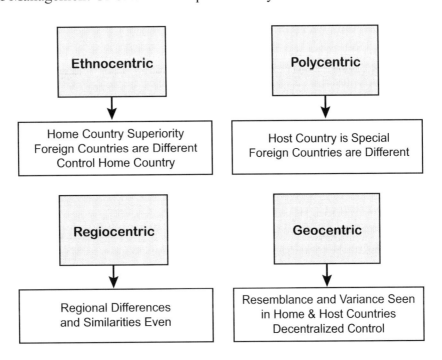

Economic Environment: Deals with the availability of capital, rate of interest, labor availability and how well they are organized, general price levels, the degree of productivity, the willingness of entrepreneurs and availability of Managerial skills.

Technological Environment: How good the available knowledge is used through technology is a factor to reckon with. How to conceive ideas, how to design, how to produce optimally, how to effect efficient distribution and how well marketing is done, are all questions that are technology-oriented.

Social Environment: This is the value systems unique to a particular group of people or society. The value system consists of attitudes, behavioral pattern, needs, wants, expectations, levels of education, the degree of intelligence, general beliefs, customs and traditions followed by a particular group of people or society.

Political and Legal Environment: This consists mainly of laws, rules, regulations, governmental policies, etc., that directly affect an organization. Managers are to act within the laws of the land, follow the rules and regulations faithfully, and in case of a change in policy that has a direct bearing on the enterprise, to act accordingly.

Ethical Environment: Longman Advanced American Dictionary describes (1) "Ethics" and (2) "Ethical" as: (1) "…the study of the moral rules and principles of behavior in society, and how they influence the choices people make…," and, (2) "…relating to principles of what is right and what is wrong…" Ethical Environment therefore means holding on to moral principles, guided by value systems prevalent in society and generally behaving in a responsible way.

Social Responsibilities: Organizations as well as managers should be socially responsive to the society as a whole and should be able to do their bit when a situation calls for it. They should be seen as contributing members of solutions to the social problems.

Functional Management

PLANNING

Planning comprises of setting objectives i.e., goals for the organization as well as developing work-maps that identify the ways and means of achieving such objectives. It is the most basic function of managing and all other functions are built, brick by brick, over it. Broadly speaking it revolves around the selection of not only the total organizational objectives, but departmental, even sectional goals, and more importantly spelling out in clear terms the ways through which such objectives, goals are to be accomplished. What? How? When and Who? are decided in advance at the planning stage. What to do, How to do, When to do and Who exactly will do is the primary objective of good planning. It, therefore, precedes all other managerial functions. Since planning and controlling are related most intricately they become inseparable and therefore, a good plan always spells out yardsticks for accomplishing the planned objective. It is obvious control measures are also part and parcel of a well thought out plan.

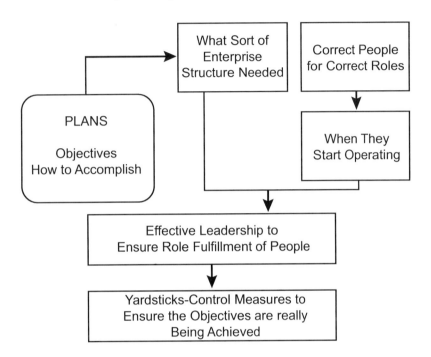

TYPES OF PLANS

- **Mission Statement:** What is the main purpose of the company? The purpose of a University is primarily teaching and then doing research on studies. Every organization's principal planning document gives its mission statement explaining what the organization stands for and what its activities are going to be. Example: The mission statement of DuPont has been spelled out as "…better living through chemistry…"

- **Objectives**: Objectives are identified goals of an organization towards accomplishment of which all organizational activities are directed. It is an action program specifying what should be achieved over a specified time and what resources are to be employed in achieving such objectives. What is an organization going to do in terms of business, i.e., what business it is aiming at and how it is going about it? What is the time frame, what are the resources and where from they are coming, who all are going to be responsible and who all are accountable for achieving the spelled out objectives? These points are to be clearly considered.

- **Policies**: A policy can be defined as a predetermined action course that serves as a guide for the identified and accepted objectives and goals. A policy indicates the management strategy towards attainment of the overall objectives and goals and seeks to establish a platform of guiding principles, which makes delegation of work to lower levels easy.

- **Procedures and Rules**: They can be defined as guides to action. In order to handle future activities one needs a plan that shows clearly what methods are to be used. And this plan that establishes such methods is known as procedure. Procedures are available at every level of an organization. This method is more widely adhered to in the lower levels. Some organizations have even departmental procedures cogently spelled out for the people of the department to follow. Rules give us distinct action plans without permitting any sort of discretion whatsoever. The action plan may spell out what action or non-action is to be taken in clear terms. They are very simple plans.

- **Programs**: Programs contain a simple, complicated or complex plan of activities developed primarily for carrying out stated policies. It simplifies the process of decision-making. A program generally consists of objectives, policies, procedures, rules, individual task allocations, what action or inaction to be taken or not taken by whom and when, and what resources are to be employed in order to successfully carry out a specified goal. Programs are also assisted by appropriate budgets in quantity or dollar terms.

- **Budgets**: Budgets are statements of targeted results reduced to quantifiable terms. An operating budget is a "profit plan." A territory budget spells out what the target is for the territory in terms of dollars and what will be the total resources to be spent in order to achieve that quantified (in dollar terms) target. A budget is seen as a tool of control. If an organization has variable output levels, they normally have flexible/variable budgets.

STEPS IN PLANNING

1. Analysis of Opportunities: Thorough knowledge of the plus points of your company and the products, market knowledge, knowledge on competition and knowledge as to what exactly the needs and aspirations of the customer are in so far as the products are concerned.

2. Setting of Objectives: An unambiguous objective that spells out clearly where the organization is at the moment and why, where it should be heading, what should be the best direction to get there, what specific action should be taken by whom and when, and what measures should be watched to get information on whether the plan is going on the right track and at the right speed.

3. To identify the basis: The plan has to work in what sort of environment – both external and internal. To take note of all factors that form part of the external environment.

4. To identify, analyze, compare and choose the best of available alternatives.

5. To design relevant plans that are supportive in nature such as purchasing capital goods, purchasing materials, sub-assemblies and components, recruiting, training and placing needed personnel, etc.

6. Quantify for control: reduce your actions into numbers – in other words work out budgets. Example: volume of business both in quantity and dollar terms for the targeted period, inventory, operating expenses, expenditure on capital goods, sales territory budgets, etc.

There are long term plans such as a 10 year or a 5 year plan which reflects the continuity of policy and short term plans like an annual plan that sets targets for the year to be achieved and which, for the sake of control, is further bifurcated into half yearly, quarterly and even monthly plans.

DECISION MAKING

The central pith, the core of planning is decision making. There are alternatives available. Choosing the best alternative from a plethora of available alternatives and sticking to it is the focus of decision-making.

In decision-making you have to identify the Limiting Factor, which can be defined as something that stands in the way of achieving a goal. The impediment. Identify the limiting factor or factors and solve them in order to arrive at the best possible decision. How to evaluate alternatives? There are Marginal Analysis Models and Cost-effective Analysis Models. The Marginal Analysis deals in analyzing the additional units of revenue one gets from incurring a certain unit of additional costs. The cost-effective analysis deals in cost-benefit analysis, i.e., the ratio of benefits to costs. Your experience, ability to experiment and an analytical bent of mind helps you to arrive at a rational decision under specific given circumstances. Operations Research lends a scientific aura to management decision-making. There are goals, models, variables, limitations – all such factors are built into quantifiable mathematical terms or formulae to decipher and arrive at the best decision possible under a given circumstance. Not all the managers are equipped mathematically to decide among alternative solutions. It is sometimes difficult to quantify a factor. In such cases operations research can do little about it. There is Risk Analysis, which again is a method steeped in mathematical terms – it tells you what probabilities are there to arrive at decisional outcomes. There are Decision Trees, which again are statistical models which tell us which are the possible decision points, chance events which are likely to occur and what probabilities are there for each course of action. Then there is Preference Theory, which tells you a given manager's willingness to take or refrain from taking (unwillingness) risks.

CHANGE

Change is the essence of life. There are different levels of changes.

At the personal level knowledge changes are the easiest to make. Once you read this book you will have gained a little more knowledge than you had before starting it. Attitudinal change is not as difficult as individual behavior change, though time and conscious effort is needed. Group behavior change is a little more difficult than individual behavior change. Group behavior change affects an organization. If people as a group within an organization demand certain things, say, increased rest periods, lesser number of work hours, it impacts the organization and the Personnel Manager has to deal with such a situation. At the organizational level, environmental changes – Social, Economic, Political, Legal – any changes in any of the components, are going to affect the organization adversely. In the case of technological change, an organization has to face the music if it does not adapt itself to the changes adeptly and with speed. A change is certainly a limiting factor in the planning process. Rapid changes more especially in the environmental and technological areas impact organizational plans adversely. In the field of computers, the chip capacity of the hard disks increased in breathtaking speed. A 2-Gigabyte hard disk is considered obsolete – as there are 40 and 80 GB hard disks available. Again, the increase in speed of chips is breathtaking! Once radios used bulky, noisy, inelegant, vacuum tubes, which became obsolete after Bell laboratories designed transistors! In such rapidly changing, highly competitive environment, it is your own creativity and techniques bordering on innovation that are necessary to exist. Fast adaptability to change is the key.

ORGANIZING

Organizing defines organizational roles to be played by individuals, their positions and the authority relationships. Every role should be clearly defined with distinct objectives in mind. The major duties to be performed by individuals, how responsibilities are to be delegated and with what authority are all definitions to be included in the organizing process. Should also indicate what resources are available, and what information and tools are necessary to carry out such roles effectively. This is organizing in a nutshell. A formal organization is what we have seen above. An informal organization according to Chester Barnard is any joint personal activity without conscious joint purpose, even though possibly contributing to joint results. The relationships in an informal organization never reflect in any organizational chart. There may be sub-assembly groups, stress groups or accounts groups, i.e., groups of individuals. However, each group identifies itself as a contributing member and acts in unison where the group's ideal or any given member's identity or right is challenged.

ORGANIZATIONAL THEORIES

Many theorists propounded a number of theories of which the following 3 are important: (1) Classical Organization Theory (2) The Mechanistic Theory and (3) The System Theory. The <u>Classical Organizational Theory</u> deals in specializing job assignments, works towards easy managerial functions, seeks to establish authority structures and delegation of responsibility and authority, maintains bureaucracy which speaks of offices and roles, and institutes formal channels of communication among members of different departments in the organization. It deals in division of labor, vertical and horizontal specialization, scalar authority, etc.

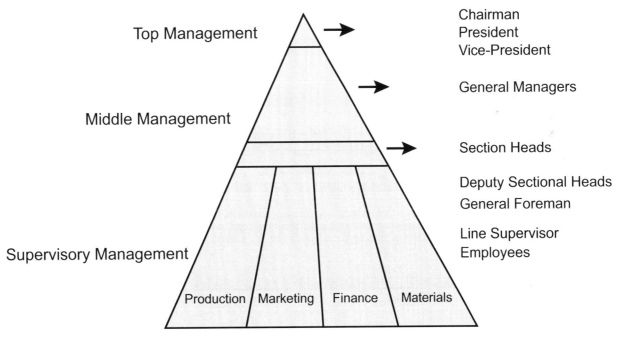

VERTICAL AND HORIZONTAL SPECIALIZATION

<u>The Mechanistic Theory</u> states that organizational change is inevitable and that organizations and people within the organizations have no other choice except following natural law. Industrialization brought in its wake a laissez faire philosophy in political

circles, which advocated the integrity or virtue of letting the natural process take its own course. This theory was supported by economic philosophy prevalent at that time. In a way it is a precursor to the later scientific management movement. The theorists had foreseen the potency of competition. They thought specialization was a tool for obtaining competitive advantage. The later versions of this theory harp on compensation structures. Both the classical organizational and the Mechanistic theories took people for granted. This gradually created uncertainties in the minds of workers and opposition started. This situation necessitated bringing focus on people. Unions and collective bargaining were begun. Human relations principles were born out of necessity. Approximately 30% of the U.S. workforce is unionized.

The Systems Theory deals with interdependence instead of independence of variables and their interactions. It started with a more intensive, very broad, wide-angle – involving a number of variables to measure complex inter-relationships – and inclusive viewpoint. Group behavior is seen in the system as broadly shaped and influenced. There are various elements in an organizational system but the common choice of an element is the individual in an organization. It identifies the system as changing, evolving and most dynamic. The systems model recognizes the environment of the system and other related variables, which includes all other subsystems, and seeks to elucidate an adequate explanation of organizational behavior. The system as a whole is seen as an open system.

ORGANIZATIONAL STRUCTURES

Any formal organization can be described as an intentional structure of roles. For the sake of functionality, a formal organizational structure is divided into many departments on the basis of their functions. There may be an Accounts department, a Marketing department, a Production department, a Material department, an Engineering department and so on. A department typically has a Head or Boss followed by a Deputy and then the assisting employees. In such a scenario, the roles of the Department Head, the Deputy and the assisting employees should be very clear and the authority relationship should be spelled out. The cooperation of all the people making up a department should be effective in order to achieve the overall organizational objectives. How many people can a department head or his deputy effectively control is the crux of the "Span" of management. There are two types – (1) Narrow Span, and (2) Wide Span.

Structure
An Organization with a Narrow Span

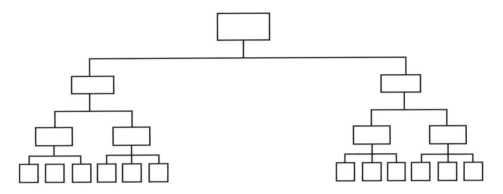

Structure
An Organization with a Wide Span

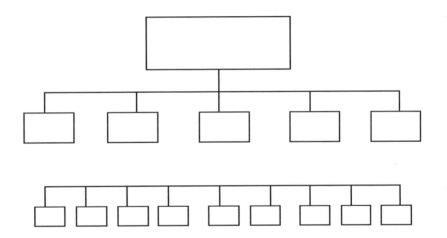

In a narrow span organizational structure, close supervision is possible, good control, and communication between Department Head and subordinates occur quickly. The disadvantage is that the super is closely involved in the subordinate's work – delegation is missing. There are many levels of management necessitating increased cost to the organization.

In a broad span organizational structure delegation becomes essential. There is a possibility of a superior losing control of subordinates. Managerial effectiveness dictates placing high quality managers. Delegation of responsibility along with requisite authority is the crux of broad span organizational structure.

AUTHORITY

In order to achieve company objectives and to sail smoothly on the chosen direction towards that objective, the superiors need authority to enforce compliance of company policies, procedures and rules by subordinates. 'Scalar' authority is identified with rank, position, as well as title.

LINE AND STAFF AUTHORITY

They are identified with relationships and not departments. In Line Authority a superior is directly responsible for the organizational actions of a subordinate. It entails making decisions and acting upon them. Staff Authority is limited only to the extent of giving counsel/advice. The advice given by Staff Authority is not binding on Line Authority.

LINE AND FUNCTIONAL AUTHORITY

Functional Authority is the right of people in other departments (i.e., other than one's own) to control selected policies, practices, procedures, processes or other functional matters with the sole aim of accomplishing set organizational goals.

DELEGATION OF AUTHORITY

The idea behind delegation is to make organizing easy. A collective effort is the key to success in an organization. Delegation of Authority happens when a super-ordinate bestows on a subordinate discretion to make decisions in the best interest of the orga-nization. It can be specific to perform a task or a cluster of tasks, or general, written or unwritten. It is also possible for the super-ordinate to revoke the delegated authority any time.

UNITY OF COMMAND

The reporting relationship of a subordinate will be smooth and effective if it is to a single superior. If an employee has to report to more than one superior then confusion, inefficiency, lack of control and total chaos prevail. A subordinate reporting to a single superior is unity of command in its simplest definition.

CENTRALIZATION AND DECENTRALIZATION

In centralization all authority is concentrated at the top. In decentralization, decision making is widely dispersed. A decentralized authority, if it is re-centralized or to put it simply, if all the authority dispersed is revoked and centralized again, it is called Re-centralization of authority.

A Centralized Authority

A Decentralized Authority

ORGANIZATION CHARTS

Functional grouping of a manufacturing organization:

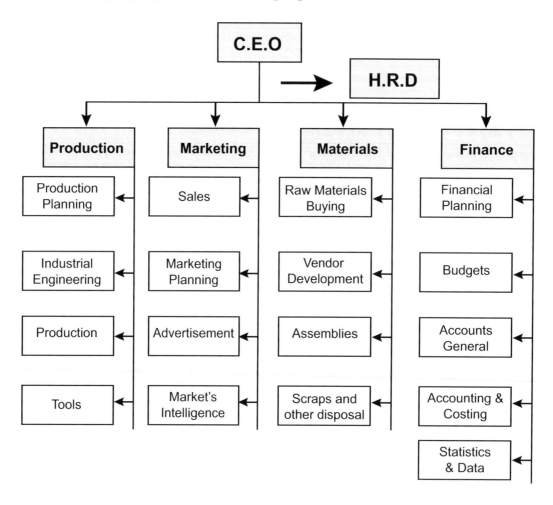

Territorial grouping of a manufacturing organization:

Market-oriented grouping of an organization:

STAFFING

In organizing we have seen authority structures, broad departmentalization, delegation, etc. In other words we have a structure and we need people to fill up the structures to do meaningful jobs. Staffing, therefore, is a systematic and methodical filling up of positions in an organizational structure by identifying total manpower requirements, recruitment, selection, placement, appraisal, promotion, training and compensation. Organizing and staffing are closely linked.

Staffing

DIRECTING

Directing = Leadership + Motivation + Communication. Directing is the process that seeks to influence people towards spontaneous and willing accomplishment of overall organizational objectives. Let us consider the components of Directing.

LEADERSHIP

Peter F. Drucker, the Modern Management philosopher and guru states in his book "The Practice of Management" "…The successful organization has one major attribute that sets it apart from unsuccessful organizations: dynamic and effective leadership…" Again, George R Terry, in his wonderful book "Principles of Management" points out that: "…Of every one hundred new business establishments started, approximately fifty, or one half, go out of business within two years. By the end of five years, only one third of the original one hundred will still be in business…" Almost all the failures were attributed to <u>ineffective leadership</u>. This tells us in clear and unambiguous terms all about leadership. In other words, the core of leadership is accomplishment of goals <u>with</u> and <u>through</u> people. Every leader has a style. The style of leaders is the consistent behavior patterns that they exhibit when they seek to influence people in order to accomplish organizational goals. The style is the consistent perception of the followers/subordinates of the leader and not the leader's perception itself.

Q = Quadrant

Q1 = Telling stage where the leader perceives the subordinates maturity level as immature. Here he spells out clearly every task.

Q2 = Selling stage where the leader perceives the maturity level of his subordinates as moderate. Here he just gives what is expected and he would like the task done.

Q3 = Participating stage where the leader perceives the subordinate to be fairly matured and invites him to participate in decisions.

Q4 = Delegating stage were the leader thinks that the subordinate to be fully matured to take on responsibilities. He only gives a broad outline and leaves the execution to the subordinate.

There are despotic leaders who only demand what they want normally in high decibels, and encourage no initiative. They are task leaders. On the other side of the spectrum you have leaders who value human relationships, who are polite but firm with subordinates, encourage initiative and are willing to share responsibilities.

Many leaders **empower** their employees by allowing them to make their own decisions and/or giving them authorization to do certain behaviors to help a customer.

MOTIVATION

William James of Harvard University conducted research on Motivation. His findings are noteworthy. He found that hourly employees whose work pattern he studied could hold on to their jobs, if they performed at 20 to 30% of their ability. His studies further elucidated that workmen can work up to 80 to 90% of their ability if they are highly motivated! In other words if the employees are highly motivated their work ability jumps from 20-30% to 80-90%!

For some money can be a good motivator. For some others safety, i.e., security, job-satisfaction, congenial atmosphere, social needs, esteem needs and self-actualization needs are important. Challenge in one's job is a motivation for some people. Rewards for accomplishments are also a motivator.

COMMUNICATION

In communication there is a sender and a receiver. If the sender sends information (message) to the receiver and if the information is understood in full by the receiver, you have communicated successfully. The main purpose of communication in an organizational setting is to influence action aimed at achieving the common goals of the organization.

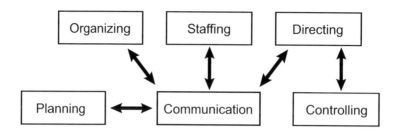

Communication is a very important factor in effective leadership and management. Not only the leaders (superiors) but also the followers (subordinates) should be adept in communicating.

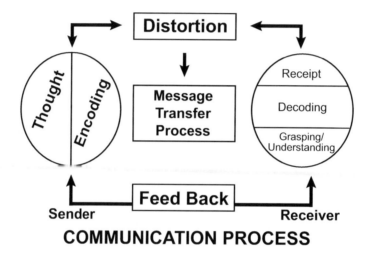

In an organization there are upward and downward communication, horizontal communication and diagonal communication.

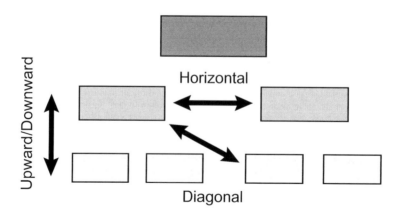

Communication/information flow in an organizational setting

Communication can be oral, written or non-verbal. When a message is repeated through various media, the comprehension and recall of that message is high with the receiver of such message. Simple words, using personal pronouns, adding graphs or graphics, short sentenced paragraphs, logical, cohesive and cogent presentation, and avoiding verborrhea will ensure good communication.

GROUP DYNAMICS

This is one of the training techniques used in organizations. Group dynamics works with role playing coupled with simulation which seeks to emphasize group behavior, how groups influence decision making and how inter-group rivalry or conflicts affect organizational effectiveness. Participants discuss team development, team member hygiene, issues that are construed as disruptive and team health.

PROBLEM SOLVING

Of all the skills a manager is expected to possess, analytical and problem solving abilities are most important. There are broadly 3-skills associated with managing. They are (1) Conceptual skills, (2) Human relation skills and (3) Technical skills.

For Top Management
Less technical, more conceptual and a good deal of human skills

For Middle Management
More of technical and conceptual skills and a good deal of human skills

Supervisory Management
More of technical, less of conceptual skills and a good deal of human skills

(Originally developed by Robert L. Katz
in Harvard Business Review - 1955)

For all the levels – Top, Middle and Supervisory, the emphasis is Human skills. "...I will pay more for the ability to deal with people than any other ability under the sun..." said John D. Rockefeller, one of the great American entrepreneurs. Managers should be ever vigilant to identify problems as they arise, analyze and track the core issue and then solve the problem by addressing the core issue and exploiting the opportunities present. Opportunities are always present in every possible threat.

CONFLICT RESOLUTION

Ask yourself, what is the conflict all about? What are the causes of the conflict? What are the possible solutions? And, what is the best of the possible solutions? Is the solution acceptable to all? Yes means you have resolved the conflict.

In an organizational backdrop, if the individual and group goals are seen as close to the organizational goals, there is bound to be an integration of goals, which satisfies all concerned.

Goals of management

Goals of organization

Goals of subordinates

Degree of accomplishment

Here there is an integration of goals. By working for the organizational goals, the Manager and subordinates reckon that they realize their own goals as well

In psychological terms conflict arises when frustration develops. The blocking or stymieing of goal accomplishment is known as frustration. In an organization conflicts arise mainly because the people in the organization have not understood their roles, assignments, tasks as well as those of their co-workers. You can educate people by having proper organization charts, authority structures, clear-cut job descriptions and job specifications, together with specific goals. Job enrichment and job rotation are also helpful

CONTROLLING

In every organization, the top management sets out the overall company objectives, departmental targets, etc., for the managers and their team of people to accomplish during a given period of time. Managers use many tools to ensure the targeted objectives are realized effectively and efficiently. Controlling, in its larger perspective, involves the measurement of activities of subordinates in order to know whether the organizational targets are realized as per plans and if there happens to be a lagging behind, what corrective actions are to be taken to ensure 100% achievement. There are 4 elements in a control system:

MANAGEMENT BY OBJECTIVES – MBO

Introduced by Peter F. Drucker (The Practice of Management) and popularized by Messrs George Odiorne and John Humbe, this participative approach is good for goal setting as well as control. The superior and the subordinates of an organization jointly identify its common goals – this is the first step. Then they define each individual team member's major areas of responsibility, which is considered on the basis of results, expected of the individual – this is the second step. And using these measures as a sort of guide to run the organization as well as appraising each individual team member's contribution – this is the third step.

NORMAL STANDARDS IN PRACTICE

Standards fall within the following types: 1) Physical Standards, 2) Capital Standards, 3) Revenue Standards, 4) Cost Standards, 5) Intangible Standards, and 6) Goals standardized for verification.

Physical Standards: Quantified standards at the operating level. Products produced in numbers, in value, material used in weightage and value, labor employed in house and in value, services rendered in value, etc.

Capital Standards: Physical items and monetary value pertaining to the capital goods used in production.

Revenue Standards: Giving monetary values to realized sales.

Cost Standards: Monetary value for the cost of operations, such as machine-hour-costs, cost of material per unit, cost of labor per unit, cost per unit of sales, etc.

Intangible Standards: These relate to human efforts and for these, it is difficult to allot a standardized measurement value.

BUDGETS – AN IMPORTANT CONTROL TECHNIQUE

Budgets are plans for a specific future period of time given in numerical or value terms. They are anticipated results in value terms of a given plan. There are cash budgets, revenue/expense budgets, materials budgets, products budgets, capital expenditure budgets, etc.

MANAGERIAL CONTROL TOOLS (MILESTONE BUDGETS)

Gantt Charts: There are many types of Gantt charts in vogue. They may be called a particular type of bar chart and the measuring unit invariably is time. For example, a progress chart – here the planned target is compared with the actual accomplishment:

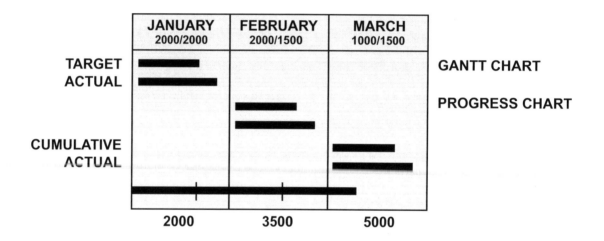

Means Chart: This is used in statistical quality control situations.

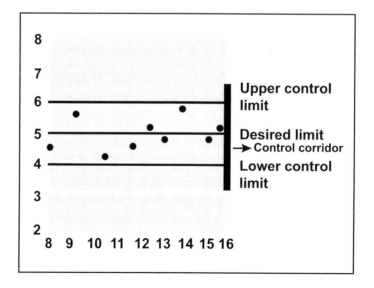

Pert (Program evaluation and review technique) and CPM (Critical Path Method):

NASA used these techniques extensively in its space programs. A project's most probable time of completion can be worked out through these techniques. Let us see an organization's budget preparation in Pert form:

Job	Description	Time Required
a	Forecasting sales	10 days
a	Market research on pricing structures of competitor	4 days
b	Sales valuing	4 days
c	Production schedules	6 days
d	Costing of production	5 days
e	Budget preparation	8 days

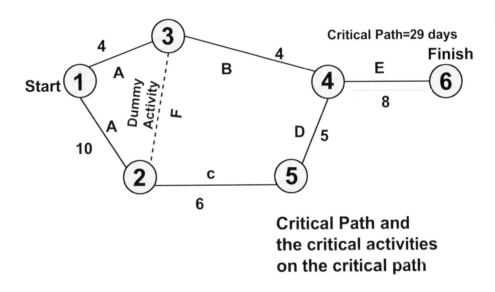

Critical Path and the critical activities on the critical path

The above is a very simple pert chart. However, such charts are prepared by giving a most pessimistic time, a most optimistic time, and a most probable time. These can then be reduced into the following formula for easy calculation.

Weightage:

t_o = optimistic time – equally likely to occur
t_p = pessimistic time – equally likely to occur
$4t_m$ = most probable time = 4 times more likely to occur than t_o, t_p.
t_e = time expected

Formula: $t_e = t_o + 4t_m + t_p / 6$

You have to arrive at standard deviation $S_t = t_p - t_o / 6$, which is one sixth of the difference between two extreme time estimates. Since standard deviation is the square root of any given distribution, we calculate variance from $V_t = (t_p - t_o / 0)2$ using probability distribution, and thus we can say expected duration of a project.

A dummy job takes only zero time for performance but it is used to show the precedence relationship. <u>Critical path</u> may be defined as the longest path in the network. Jobs (activities) throughout the critical paths are known as <u>critical jobs</u>, or <u>critical activities</u>.

Small Business, Entrepreneurship, Forms of Business and Franchise

It's the great American dream to open and run your own business. This dream is coming true for many Americans through their own ideas, purchasing a business or purchasing a franchise.

A sole proprietorship is when you own a business yourself. You have a great deal of responsibility like with any business but you carry a lot of personal risk as well. The debts of the business are also considered to be your debts. For example, if you are a sole proprietor of a restaurant and you decide to close the business while still having debts, you are personally responsible to pay those debts. If you fail to do so, creditors can sue to seize your property, like your house.

A general partnership is when a business is owned between two or more people. Like a sole proprietorship, the partners are liable for all business debts. The partnership is dissolved when one partner dies or withdraws.

A joint venture is created with a specific project in mind. This partnership dissolves when completed.

A limited partnership is made up of general partners and limited partners. General partners take care of the day-to-day running of the business while limited partners only contribute capital. The legal ramifications are different for each type of partner. The limited liability partner only risks his initial capital investment while the general partner has full legal liability.

A limited liability partnership (LLP) is created to protect partners from liability caused by other partners. An LLP is more informal than a corporation and receives partnership tax treatment.

Limited liability companies (LLC) are popular because they give you both the limited liability of a corporation and the favorable taxation of a partnership. An LLC is a separate legal entity so no member has personal liability.

A corporation is a separate legal entity. It may also be known as a C corporation. This business must be set-up with the state, usually with the help of an attorney. A corporation is owned by shareholders. It is also managed by the board of directors. Because some of the work involved in a corporation can be time consuming and administrative, including annual meetings, issuing stock, taking minutes, etc., many individuals elect to have these duties handled by professionals.

An "S" corporation is when an individual's tax returns show income generated or losses accrued by the corporation. Converting to an "S" corporation affects the tax status but does not generally effect the legal protection offered by the corporation.

Doing Business As or DBA is a way to have a fictitious name for your company or any other name than your company name.

A franchise is a ready-made business that you can purchase. You pay franchise fees, annual fees as well as a portion of your profits to the franchise. Besides all that money, you must conform to their way of doing business. While this can seem like a great way to start a business, once you get your feet wet in running the business day-to-day there will be items you want to add to your store or a different way you want to see things done. With a franchise, most of the time, that won't be possible. Part of a franchise is brand integrity. If you walk into a McDonalds in Alaska, you should get the same menu of the McDonalds in California with the same "great taste." That's what makes a franchise good, you can rely on quality. BUT this is only great for the customer. Franchise fees can be very expensive, most in the range of $100,000 and up for most businesses, and that is just for the right to have the franchise. Add to that supply costs, building and labor costs and your total capital outlay is very expensive. When you come down to it, purchasing a franchise is just purchasing yourself a job, but a job where you have to work twice as hard to make money. You are better off opening your own business from scratch or investing in other ventures. Other examples of franchise businesses are Subway, Pizza Hut, and Jiffy Lube.

The SBA or Small Business Administration was created in 1953. This government agency not only counsels new business owners but can help get loans, find locations for a new business and help with many other business issues.

Business Ethics

Business ethics are basically a collection of principles and codes of conduct that affect the way companies do business. This is a collection of right and wrong factors – which can be hard to determine in a business environment. It's challenging to balance what's good for the company with what's good for the customer.

What is ethical? Employee privacy is a large area of concern currently. Monitoring email, phone calls, typing speed, credit history for new applicants, etc., are all potential ethical dilemmas. What is the right answer?

Whistleblowing is when an employee reports to the media or the government about a company's wrong doings.

Other business ethical dilemmas are false advertising, cooking the books or making sales numbers appear better than they are.

Financial Management

Financial management is an important part of any manager's job. It's important to understand how your department contributes to the bottom line and you need to be able to understand that impact through finance.

Debt financing is the use of borrowed funds. Equity financing is the provision of funds by the owners of the business. This could include the company issuing stock to raise capital or through depreciation. Depreciation is an expense item that is deducted from revenue although it does not immediately need an outlay of cash. Maturity is the amount of time until a debt must be paid. Leverage is when you use borrowed money to earn more money than the amount of interest paid on the funds. For example, any business owner can use the concept of leverage. If a baker borrows $1000 to buy a new stove that will allow him to make more money than the $1000+interest, he is using leverage.

Deregulation is the reducing or elimination of laws regarding how an industry does business. A good example would be most of the utilities in the U.S.

Working capital is a firm's investment in their assets. An example would be the baker's over.

What are other examples of assets a company could have?
• Equipment
• Capital (money)
• Accounts Receivables (invoices out to customers for work that has been completed)
• Inventory
• Prepaid expenses (such as a year of pre-paid medical insurance)

New working capital is current assets minus liabilities. What are some examples of liabilities?
• Accounts Payable
• Notes Payable
• Payroll
• Outstanding vacation hours/pay

Liquidity is a company's ability to make payments that are due. If the baker needs to pay his employees $1500 and only has $1600 in the bank, he is not very liquid. Liquid can also refer to the ease of transferring other assets such as inventory into ready cash.

Short term fund sources generally come from these areas:
1. Trade Credit. For example, when the baker buys flour from his supplier and doesn't pay until he's sold his bread – no bank is involved, just the supplier and the baker.

2. Factoring. This is when a business sells its accounts receivables to a financial institution at a discount. The baker sells bread to a supermarket and is owed $2000. To get cash quickly to pay for upcoming expenses and payroll, the baker could sell this invoice to a bank or individual for $1800. This means that the baker gets $1800 today and the factor (a.k.a. the bank or person who just bought the accounts receivables) has to get the supermarket to pay. The factor will get $200 for his trouble, which is usually not much hassle.

3. Commercial Bank Loans. This is a standard loan from a bank.

4. Line of Credit. This is a credit agreement with a bank to pay it off in a short period of time. Another form of a line of credit would be a revolving credit where the borrower could pay it off over a period of time while accruing interest. Credit cards are revolving credit accounts.

Promissory note is a written promise by a customer to pay a sum of money and interest to the supplier or payee at a certain date.

A certified check is a check certified by a bank to have funds backing the check. This guarantees that the check will not bounce. A cashier's check is very much like a certified check with the exception that the bank is the guarantor of the funds on the check, where a certified check is on an individual's account.

Treasury Bills are a government obligation which matures in 91, 182 or 365 days. Treasure Notes are a government obligation which matures between 1-7 years. Treasure Bonds are a government obligation which matures in a specified period of time over 7 years.

Merger is the act of joining two companies. Acquisition is the purchase of another company. Venture capitalist is a person or an organization that invests money in a company for a part of the profits.

Securities

The securities market is basically the buying and selling of stocks and bonds. A stock split is when a company gives each shareholder more shares. If you own 500 shares of eBay and they have a stock split, you will now have 1000 shares. A cash dividend is a payment to shareholders. A stock dividend is when that payment is paid in stock instead of cash.

Over-the-counter market is a network of dealers that trade unlisted securities. A new company that is preparing to go public or have its IPO, Initial Public Offering, must first reveal certain business details to via prospectus to the SEC or Securities Exchange Commission.

Speculative trading is the buying and selling of securities in hope of near-term changes in pricing. Sometimes investors do not pay for their stock right away. They are allowed to borrow part of the money from their broker. Margin is the price that must be paid in cash.

Short selling is a strategy you can use if stock prices are falling. Short selling involves selling shares you don't own to a buyer. A put option is an option to sell a specific stock at a specific price and time in the futures. A call option is an option to buy a stock at a specific price and time in the future.

An index fund is a mutual fund made up of a group of stocks that mimic the S&P 500. The S & P stands for Standard and Poor's.

Risk Management

There are four ways to deal with risk:

1. Assuming the risk – setting aside enough money to pay for potential losses
2. Minimizing the risk – screening employees, network passwords, etc.
3. Avoiding the risk – avoiding certain industries (i.e., lumberjacking)
4. Shifting the risk – purchasing insurance policies

COBRA stands for The Comprehensive Omnibus Budget Reconciliation Act. It requires employers to allow employees to retain medical insurance after they quit or are terminated, for up to 18 months.

Computer Hardware and Hardware Functions

The term computer **hardware** refers to any of the electronic components that make up the computer such as the monitor, the CPU, the disk drives, or the printer. Hardware is separate from **software**, which is the general term for any program that performs calculations and controls what you see on the monitor. A computer comes with some basic software when it is purchased; this software is known as the operating system. An **operating system (OS)** is a master control program that oversees all the functions of the computer and manages the way in which information is placed onto the various hardware devices. Microsoft Windows is an example of a popular operating system.

The computer's **CPU** or **central processing unit** is the main microprocessor that controls the computer. Most personal computers (PC's) are powered by microprocessors that are manufactured by Intel, such as a Pentium or Celeron processor. The speed of the CPU determines how quickly software programs will perform their functions. There are three components to a CPU: the arithmetic logic unit, a control unit, and a set of registers.

Every computer has an **instruction set**, which is a list of keywords that corresponds to all of the operations that the CPU contains. A CPU can be a **complex instruction set computer (CISC)** that supports approximately 100 instructions for greater speed or a **reduced instruction set computer (RISC)** with a minimal set of instructions designed for a specialized application. **Registers** are specialized storage areas that store values while the instructions operate upon them. The **arithmetic logic unit (ALU)** is the component of the CPU that supports the standard arithmetic functions like add and subtract as well as logical operations like AND and OR. The **control unit** is the electronic controller over the operations that the instructions perform much like the brain controls our actions.

 # Computer Devices

Another critical hardware device is the **hard disk** or disk drive. The hard disk is an electronic component of the computer that is used for storing information and may also be called a **hard drive**. The hard disk offers **RAM memory**, which means information can be read from and written to this device. RAM memory is distinguished from **ROM** memory found in the CPU; ROM memory is read-only. It makes sense that parts of the operating system are read-only; that is, nothing else can be written over the basics of the operating system. If the operating system is destroyed, the computer will no longer operate properly.

The hard disk is an integral part of the computer and is portable only to the extent that the computer itself is portable, such a notebook or laptop PC. Alternate drives are available to handle portable information storage devices such as **floppy disks, diskettes** or **CD's**. Floppy disks are portable storage devices that are 5.25 inches and mostly out-of-date today while diskettes are 3.5 inches wide and are encased in plastic. CD's or **compact disks** are the latest in portable information devices. All of the storage devices can be divided into **files**, which represent individual documents or other collections of information that are identified by unique names.

The computer user communicates with the software and CPU by entering information through a **keyboard**, which is called an **input device** because it is used to enter information into the computer. The keyboard provides alphabetic, numeric, punctuation, symbols and control keys. When a key is depressed, an electronic signal that is unique to the key is sent to the CPU. The operating system typically displays the associated letter, number or symbol on the **monitor**, which is a piece of hardware that resembles a television screen. The computer user also enters information by using a communication device known as a **mouse.** A mouse is another input device. This device fits easily in the human hand and is designed to roll on a flat surface that roughly translates to the monitor's area. The mouse is used to locate an area on the monitor that the user is interested in. Clicking the buttons on the mouse is a typical method for selecting options that are displayed on the monitor by software programs.

The keyboard, monitor and mouse are the primary peripheral devices that are used for entering information into the computer. A **peripheral device** is any electronic component that is attached to the computer but external to it. Another external peripheral device is a **scanner**, which is used to copy paper documents or pictures into memory on the hard drive. A touch screen is another input device that is used in applications that are available to a general user. The **touch screen** enters the user's choices based upon a simple pressing of the indicated area of the pressure-sensitive panel. **Bar code readers** are used in business applications to interpret bar codes that indicate what the product is; bar code readers are particularly important in warehousing applications. A **point-of-sale (POS) terminal** is a computerized cash register that allows the input of data such as item sold, price, and method of payment. **Digital cameras** can now be connected directly to a personal computer for downloading pictures onto the hard disk.

Just as there are a variety of peripheral devices for input, there are also numerous **output devices,** that is, components whose main purpose is to retrieve processed information that is stored in the computer's memory. The most familiar output device is a **printer**, which produces a paper copy of the desired document, picture, or graphs. Some printers are now special purpose devices that are designed only to print pictures. The computer **monitor** serves as an output device when it is used to retrieve information that is stored in memory. The **PC speakers** are also an output device for audio messages that accompany software systems or that are recorded on Internet web sites.

 # Computer Configurations

A **personal computer (PC)** is a small computer that is equipped with its own operating system and peripheral devices that are needed typically by one individual. PC's are differentiated from a **personal digital assistant (PDA)**, which is a hand-held computer that is customized for everyday functions for personal organization, such as an appointment calendar, an address book, a notepad and fax or other two-way messaging capability.

Large companies historically have relied upon some form of mainframe computer to handle their voluminous data processing needs. A **mainframe computer** is a multi-user computer capable of simultaneously processing thousands of calculations. Mainframe computers were the primary type of computers available from the 1960's onward.

DIGITAL REPRESENTATION

Computers are electronic and can only store information as a group of **binary digits** that is composed of 0's and 1's only. Each binary digit is known as a **bit.** Eight consecutive bits in computer memory are called a **byte.**

Our normal arithmetic is base 10 or decimal, with digits 0-9 only. Binary arithmetic within the computer is base 2, with digits 0-1 only. So decimal 0 is 0 binary, 1 is 1, but

2 is 10 binary, and 3 is 11 binary, 4 is 100 binary as so on. While the internal computer performs **numeric calculations** in binary, the operating system converts the internal binary to the decimal system we are accustomed to whenever the numbers are sent to an output device such as the monitor or printer. Sometimes very large numbers are stored in the computer in a form known as **binary-coded decimal (BCD)** where each decimal digit is stored as a 4-bit binary number.

How are letters or text stored? The letters that come in as electronic signals from the keyboard are converted to **Extended Binary Coded Decimal Interchange Code (EBCDIC)** for IBM mainframe computers and **American Standard Code for Information Interchange (ASCII)** for personal computers. The basic idea for these codes is that every letter of the alphabet and every other symbol, like the punctuation marks and percent sign, are converted to a binary code that fits into an 8-bit byte; however, ACSII coding uses only 7 of the 8 bits. These byte-oriented encoding schemes can handle 256 possible characters and symbols and thus are not suited for languages that have more symbols, like some of the Oriental languages.

Pictures have their own graphics digital representation or **Joint Photographic Experts Group (JPEG)** format. This format can represent up to 16.7 million color variations for each **pixel** or picture element. A pixel is the smallest picture element that an output device can handle. A picture is composed of a grid of pixels. Another picture format is **Tagged Image File Format (TIFF)** that is used for scanned photographic images. Graphs and graphics files are compressed using **Graphics Interchange Format (GIF)**. Video has its own format as well, namely the **Moving Picture Experts Group (MPEG)** format which provides for the compression of digitized videos and animation.

Accounting

Financial accounting is being able to determine exactly where a business is at financially based on their sales, income and expenses. We already know what assets and liabilities are from a few pages back. Now let's learn the basic accounting equation: Assets – Liabilities = Owner's equity (capital).

A balance sheet is a financial statement that shows the assets (left) and the liabilities (on the right). Here is an example:

Assets	Liabilities & Stockholder's Equity
Cash Accounts Receivable Inventory Prepaid Expenses Land Building Less accumulated depreciation Intangible assets (patents)	Accounts Payable Accrued Wages Estimated Tax Liabilities Bonds Payable Capital Stock Retained Earnings

A fixed asset is an asset held longer than one year. Intangible assets have no physical form – they can include patents, trade secrets, etc.

The income statement is created with the following formula:

Revenues – Expenses = Net Income

Gross profit is the difference between net sales and cost of goods sold.

International Business

Importing and exporting are how countries trade goods and services with each other. An export is produced in one country and sold to another. Exports are a small percent of GDP for the U.S. unlike for countries such as Germany and the United Kingdom. Imports are currently how we spend 20% of our money – and it is steadily increasing.

Trade barriers are anything that makes it difficult (or creates ad barrier) to trade. One natural barrier to trade is distance. This increases the cost to transport a product. Another barrier is language. If you cannot communicate with your buyer, then you cannot initiate or complete a transaction. A protectionist is someone who proclaims "buy American." Their primary aim is to keep jobs, companies and industries inside the country. Currently, there is a lot of coverage in the news about jobs being outsourced to India.

A tarrif is a duty or a tax that a government puts on products that are imported or exported from a country. Sometimes a country enacts an embargo. An embargo is a prohibition or suspension of a certain type of item, or anything from a certain country or region. For example, the U.S. has an embargo against ivory and some types of firearms. Each country chooses their own items (if any) on which to place an embargo.

GATT is the General Agreement of Tariffs and Trade is a treaty designed to reduce trade barriers. NAFTA is the North American Free Trade Agreement which helps reduce trade barriers between the United States, Canada and Mexico.

The World Bank is a part of the United Nations that provides loans to countries for development projects. IMF is the International Monetary Fund, an agency that seeks to establish a way for countries to finance and pay off loans. IMF is affiliated with the World Bank.

A bill of lading is a document of title which is a contract between the shipper and the carrier (think you and Fedex). It also serves as a receipt for the products that the shipper has placed on the carrier.

Human Resource Management

HAWTHORNE EFFECT

In 1927 a series of studies began at Western Electric Company in Hawthorne, Illinois. The first study was testing the assumption that the worker output would increase if the level of light in the plant was turned up. To test the theory, they took several female workers into a separate room in the factory and tested their output against a variety of lighting. Surprisingly, output increased regardless of the light level, until it was too dark to see and then it remained constant. Why? By taking the workers into another room at the plant, they had done something inadvertently, they had made the workers feel special. Experts coin this example to be the Hawthorne effect, which is where the interest in the people's problems effect the outcome, not the changes themselves.

THEORY X & Y

Theory X is a management approach where you believe that people dislike work and responsibility and are only motivated by money and other financial incentives. It also assumes that these people must be micro managed and supervised.

Theory Y is the assumption that all people enjoy work, and will control their own performance if you give them the chance. These people will want to do a good job and work better with a hands off approach.

PERSONNEL ADMINISTRATION

All resources in an organization need management, i.e., they are subjected to the processes of management viz., planning, organizing, directing and controlling. Building and machinery are physical resources. Stocks, bank balances are financial resources. People are human resources. While no other resource – capital, land, machines can talk back, only human resources can think and talk back and this makes management of this resource that much more difficult.

Personnel Administration is that branch of general management which: (a) looks into manpower resources of an organization (b) has a managerial function of planning, organizing, directing and controlling and an operative function of recruiting, developing, compensating, integrating human resources together with keeping records on manpower (c) aims at harmonious labor (d) aims to achieve organizational goals by integrating human resources.

The form "industrial relations" is a broader concept, which seeks to bring in harmonious relationship between labor, managements and the government of an industry.

Managing diversity is when you create a work environment where women, minorities and people with disabilities can perform and succeed on the job.

The term "labor management" normally defines the managing of manual workers of an organization. Working conditions and worker discipline together with the general recruitment, selection, compensation, etc., are dealt with by labor management.

The scope of "personnel management" is truly wider. It deals with the recruitment, selection, placement, training, compensation, working condition, etc., pertaining to all categories of personnel in an organization. Personnel administration also deals with generation of mutual trust, total co-operation and cohesive work force culture and maintaining cordial relations with trade unions.

Affirmative action is a detailed plan that a company makes to recruit women and minorities into positions and promotions. The glass ceiling is a term used to describe the attitudes and unwritten policies that have blocked women or any person from moving up the corporate ladder.

PERFORMANCE APPRAISALS

An organization's current human resources need timely evaluation of their capabilities in order to be ready for any future needs. There are two sources where managers look to appraise capabilities of human resources: (1) Personnel records (which are built on the applications submitted), and (2) Personnel Appraisal ratings. (1) Personnel records give all the data in the application together with high school, college and other educational institutional records, selection test scores, salary/wage started and changes made during the service, promotional opportunities availed, transfer effected, training courses attended, disciplinary actions, if any, recorded and personnel appraisal ratings. (2) Personnel Appraisal: The main purpose of any personnel appraisal plan is to help the employee to know his strengths and weaknesses, opportunities and threats (SWOT) and in order to build him for meeting ever increasing job challenges. Constructive criticism and helpful dialogue are excellent guidance for the employee to gain perspective and mental maturity to perform his allotted tasks skillfully and rise in the organization ladder. Companies rate many items pertaining to an individual and we give below an excerpt which will give a good idea of this concept.

Item Rated	Number of Times Found in 50 Merit-Rating Forms*
Group 1: The Old Standbys	
Quantity of work	44
Quality of work	31
Group 2: Job Knowledge and Performance	
Knowledge of job	25
Attendance	14
Punctuality	12
Safety habits	7
Good housekeeping	3
Group 3: Characteristics of the Individual	
Cooperativeness	36
Dependability	35
Initiative	27
Intelligence	17
Accuracy	14
Industry	14
Adaptability	14
Attitude	13
Personality	13
Judgment	12
Application	10

Leadership	6
Conduct	6
Resourcefulness	6
Health	5
Neatness	5
Appearance	4
Enthusiasm	4
Potential	4

*Integrity, loyalty, speech, tact and thoroughness were rated by three or fewer companies.
Source: "Marks of the Good Worker," National Industrial Conference Board Management Record, Vol. 18, No. 5 (May 1956), 168-70

Most companies have their own appraisal methods but the data normally sought to rate belongs to any one of the elements given above.

Good companies normally rate the person on the basis of his job-performance, attitude and behavior and then call the individual for personal counseling.

There are many methods of job evaluation and let us discuss some of them:

(1) <u>Ranking system</u>: In this jobs are ranked on the basis of responsibilities and duties and their importance to overall company objectives. Salary/wages are determined accordingly.

(2) <u>Classification method</u>: They define grades for requirements that are found common to various tasks on the basis of comparison between requirements regarding each task; they are classified with relevant grades.

(3) <u>Points system</u>: Requirements appropriate to each job are analyzed and quantified. Job requirements are subdivided into smaller degrees and each degree is assigned points. The total points a job gets determines its relative position vis-à-vis the job structure.

(4) <u>Factor Comparison</u>: For a few predetermined key jobs, points are allotted and wage rates for such key jobs are fixed. This will serve as a guiding factor for grading other jobs. Let us see three jobs of an organization now:

Job Requirements	Maximum Points	Maintenance Person	Machine Operator	Store Clerk
Experience	20.00	10.00	15.00	5.00
Job Knowledge and Job Skill	40.00	35.00	20.00	10.00
Negligence	20.00	15.00	10.00	5.00
Working Conditions	20.00	5.00	5.00	5.00
	100.00	65.00	50.00	25.00

The above organization fixes a basic pay of say $200 for all categories per month. In addition, the organization decides to pay $2 per point as per the above evaluation in which case the 3 job-men will receive:

	Maintenance Person $	Machine Operator $	Store Clerk $
Basic	200	200	200
Points Payment	130 (65*2)	100 (50*2)	50 (25*2)
	330.00	300.00	250.00

COLLECTIVE BARGAINING AND UNIONS

Unions are formal associations of employees formed with a view to represent employees in any dialogue to bargain collectively with the management. Their negotiations with the management include improved working conditions, better wage structures, lesser hours of work, more rest periods, etc., and generally work towards establishing good labor policies. In the USA 'organized' labor is a term normally used to distinguish members of unions from employees who do not have a formal union to support them. There are blue-collar as well as white-collar worker unions in the USA. Dale Yoder, in his magnum opus "Personnel Management and Industrial Relations," has given the following as the most widely accepted general policies of American Unions:
"...

1. *To bargain collectively and to expand and increase the scope of the collective bargaining system.*

2. *To maintain and expand the security and survival capacity of unions and their ability to withstand attacks, and to back up demands with solidarity as well as economic resources.*

3. *To gain and maintain exclusive control of labor supplies in particular labor markets as a means of enforcing union demands for what are regarded as appropriate working conditions.*

4. *To improve the economic status and welfare of union members, increasing their earnings and relative shares in national income and their influence, both in employment and in the larger societies in which they are members.*

5. *To develop and improve the union's arsenal of weapons – programs, practices and techniques to be used in conflict and defense of the organization and in expanding its power.*

6. *To represent members in the area of political action, identifying candidates and officeholders who are friendly or unfriendly, lobbying and securing political concessions for unions and their members.*

7. *To maintain a strong organization, democratically controlled but with enough internal discipline to implement such policies as have been described above.*

8. *To facilitate improved member understanding of union policies and programs and increase skill and competence on the part of union officers by appropriate educational programs…"*

TRAINING AND DEVELOPMENT

Training can be considered as a program built primarily to assist employee development. There are various kinds of training in vogue: (1) Apprenticeship (2) Refresher courses (3) Promotional training (4) On the job training (5) Off the job training, etc. The specific purposes behind training are:

(1) Knowledge and skill enhancement

(2) Makes it possible to introduce new methods. Encourages people to introduce new methods thereby making it possible for the personnel to work more effectively and efficiently.

(3) Knowledge on safety. It provides the much needed knowledge on how to operate machines without any risk.

(4) Latest techniques: Training impacts latest techniques available and makes the operator much more skillful and technique-oriented.

(5) Morale boosting: Promotes self-confidence of personnel as they are trained in skills, knowledge, aptitude and attitude necessary to do their job most efficiently.

(6) Self-actualization: It paves the way for employees to realize their full potential.

Many corporate business houses have substantial training budgets to augment and fine tune their managerial skills. On the job training for managers include:

(1) Planned progression
(2) Temporary promotion
(3) Job rotation
(4) The committee method
(5) Coaching

Training needs are to be analyzed before arriving at the training program. How is need analyzed? A hypothetical case study:

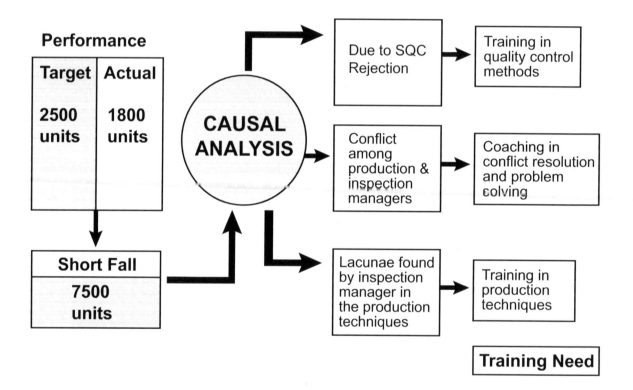

TRAINING NEED ANALYSIS

Training may consist of:

1) Coaching

2) Conference

3) Group dynamics

4) Idea tracking

5) Managerial games

6) Multimedia presentations

7) Role playing

8) Programmed learning

9) T Group

10) Workshop, and

11) Special tuition

ORGANIZATIONAL DEVELOPMENT – OD

Organizational development – simply OD – is a methodical, integrated and a well thought out and well planned approach that seeks to improve organizational effectiveness. The design generally reveals solutions to problems that threaten or are already impeding operating efficiency of the organization at all levels. It may be ineffective communication, or excessive centralization, or extreme decentralization, and/or even willful apathy amounting to non-cooperation. The solutions to problems are found in team building programs, job enrichment programs, programs meant for organizational behavior modification, or simple MBO (Management by Objective), which we have already seen.

The normal organizational development process first aims to recognize the problems correctly, then diagnoses the problems, then seeks data and information feedback, then begins designing and developing a change strategy with proper interventions and then establishes yardsticks for effective evaluation of the change.

LEGAL CONCERNS

The government's priority is to restrain unlawful activities taking over business and to regulate it in a methodical manner. This is one of the reasons why parliaments all over the world enact appropriate laws to not only safeguard the interests of business but to restrain them from unlawful activities. They contain rules to regulate business not with a view to suppress free enterprise but with a view to encourage so that they prosper in a free market. There are thousands of rules and procedures a manager has to learn and interpret of Federal government alone. Add to this the State laws, rules and procedures and you have a formidable challenge. In an Industrial setting a Manager has to learn about Factories Act and rules, Payment of Wages Act and rules, Minimum Wages Act and rules, Employee Provident Fund Acts and rules, Payment of Bonus Act and rules, Gratuity Act and rules, Industrial Disputes Act and rules, Trade Unions Act and rules, Purchase Tax Act, Sales Tax Act, Central and State Excise rules, Customs Acts and rules, Income Tax Act and rules, Value Added Tax (VAT) rules and procedures, etc. Of course, there may be legal advisers to impart correct interpretation of rules and advice on proper follow up of procedures.

Common law or case law is unwritten law that has grown out of previous judges decisions. When a lawyer cites a pre-existing finding from another court, he or she is citing case law.

Operational Aspects of Management

INFORMATION PROCESSING AND MANAGEMENT

The main managerial function is to get things done by making things happen and not piously hoping for desired results to materialize and wishing problems to evaporate. To get things done through others – the essence of managing – in an organizational backdrop requires precise informational flow for a manager. Without precise information from above and from below, a manager finds it difficult to take proper direction and provide proper action plans.

Today, thanks to the Information Technology Revolution, there is an abundant cascade of information, a veritable information system. Instead of hunting for info today we choose from among a bewildering variety of information on any subject.

A manager needs information in order to effectively focus on the functions such as planning, organizing, directing and controlling. The policies of management in the areas of inventories, customer service, scheduling, etc. are developed from information and data generated from production control functions. Likewise information on the competitors' activities, market standing, competitors' overall strategies, their offer of inducements, their planning to introduce new products, etc., are gleaned from the market by salesmen, by wholesalers, by distributors, by retailers and by friendly salesmen of competitors. Such information whether for production or for marketing is essential for managers to process, analyze and use effectively to succeed in accomplishing overall organizational objectives.

Information and data processing in an organization:

OPERATIONS PLANNING AND CONTROL

A simple illustration of Operations Management

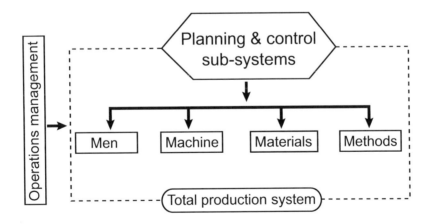

Operations Management can be defined as the planning, organizing, executing and controlling of an organization's total production system through optimal use of the factors that contribute to the planning and control subsystems, viz., Men, Machines, Materials and Methods, and in the process suggesting effective improvement for the total production system.

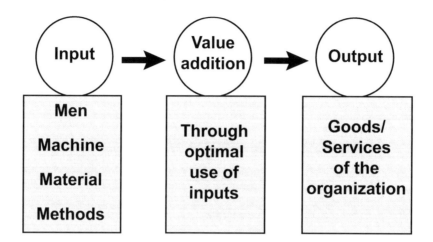

Any production system thinks in terms of excellent customer service, investment on inventory and effective utilization of resources resulting in minimal cost of plant operations. A good production control system always centers around:

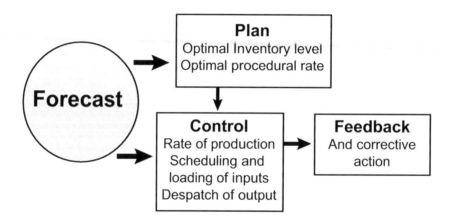

There are a few important steps in Production Planning Forecasting: (1) Preparation of essential information and data (2) Working on the forecast, and (3) Tracking the forecast.

In a factory "Lead time" means the time it takes to get an inventory item – from ordering to arrival and taking into stock. In planning production you have to take into account (a) set up time (b) production time (c) queue time (d) movement time, and (e) waiting time. A typical production plan:

PISTON – 4 STROKE (IN PIECES)

Date	Sales	Production	Inventory
Opening Balance	–	–	15,000
10/9/2000	7,000.00	8,000.00	16,000
11/9/2000	5,000.00	10,000.00	21,000
12/9/2000	10,000.00	7,000.00	18,000
13/9/2000	10,000.00	8,000.00	16,000
14/9/2000	9,000.00	9,000.00	16,000
15/9/2000	8,000.00	6,000.00	14,000
Closing Balance	–	–	14,000

Another new concept in inventory is called JIT or just in time inventory. This is the idea that you only get supplies, products and inventory right before they are needed. Walmart is a great example of using JIT inventory. Their extensive database monitors what is selling in what store and only sends exactly what each store needs, right before they run out. Walmart is also the biggest retailer in the U.S.

PRODUCTIVITY

Productivity is a very complex issue as it depends on a host of variables, some of which may not be easily predictable and therefore must be taken into account. The design of the job itself is a complex factor. Technology is another. Human and managerial facts lend more complexity. Add to these the external factors; you have an issue which is complex and sophisticated at the same time. In its rudimentary equation, productivity relates to the input-output ratio meant for a given time period. The constant factor of course is quality as there is no compromise on that score in any organization. If given expression, a productivity equation looks like the one given below:

Productivity = Output/Input

Suppose, a tailor, Mr. X, in a normal shift of 8 hours stitches 40 medium sized shirts. Mr. X's productivity 40/8 = 5 shirts per machine hour. The productivity here is measured in terms of units produced per machine hour worked. Increased effectiveness and total efficiency are the hallmarks of increased productivity.

TOTAL QUALITY MANAGEMENT (TQM)

Quality of a product determines its salability. Products enjoying exceptional quality standards demand a premium. There should be a conscious effort to maintain a high quality in not only the end product, but even the methods, systems, communication and thinking of top level to the floor level employee. A good quality program includes:

(1) Determination of standards of quality

(2) Institution of an effective continuous on the job checking program with responsibilities and accountability firmly fixed

(3) A recording system for comparing errors vs. standards

(4) A method which spells out corrective action, and

(5) To install a program of analysis and quality improvement whenever found needed.

Checking on the production line while the job is on is a good system. However, it may not be possible to check every piece produced. Here the statistical quality methods come to help. Normally checking is done on a random basis (Random Sampling Method). The most common program liked by organizations is the <u>acceptance sampling</u> method. A sample, normally 10 to 15% of a batch from a running production line, is checked. If they find that a high majority of the checked batch quantities consistently match the set standards for qualitative accuracy, the entire batch (the balance of 90 to 85% as the case may be) is accepted. This is acceptance sampling in essence.

Today there is ISO-9000 (which tells us that a well thought out system will produce predicted quality consistently, with consistency in the implementation of the system at every stage – not only in design or production but in policies and actions of all employees), TQM – Total Quality Management (which tells us to continuously meet agreed customer requirements at the lowest cost, by realizing the potential of employees). 6-Sigma Concept (which tells us that, when a product is rated as 6-Sigma, it means that the product exhibits no more than 3.4 non conformities per million opportunities (NPMO) at the part and process levels). All these concepts aim to give a zero-defect product.

The quality movement has acquired many gurus. Chief among them are: (1) Phillip B. Crosby – who always emphasized "zero-defect," (2) Dr W. Edwards Deming – who is considered the forefather of the Japanese quality revolution and the thrust of his philosophy has always been planned reduction of variation, and (3) Dr. Joseph Juran – who always thought and taught that quality is achievable through people rather than technique.

WORK SCHEDULING

An effective and most efficient production control system always assigns a prominent role to work scheduling. There are input scheduling and output scheduling. In input scheduling input control is divided into: (1) Order Selection, i.e., the right orders for feeding into the machines. This is based on planned production rate or customs order, or material control system. (2) Scheduling – after considering the operations to be performed on each production order, they allot times and arrive at the completion date. (3) Loading – this involves the working out of hours required to perform each operation and then compares that factor with availability of work hours in each cost (work) center. The capacity planning vis-à-vis the machine, operations, operator, etc., tells you what would be your job flow rate. Let us see the normal scheduling steps:

| **Provide Data** | Sequencing of operations | **Develop systems** | Scheduling procedures / Shop calendar | **Choice of scheduling method** | Forward scheduling / Backward scheduling |

In scheduling one has to: (1) multiply order quality by time per each operation. (2) To the number arrived at 1, add time of transit, and (3) provide for unexpected delays converting it to hours and add to total of 1+2.

Forward Scheduling: Starts today and works out the schedule date for each operation in order to find out the completion date for the order.

Backward Scheduling: Starts with the date on which the completed order is needed in the stores department for shipping, then works out backwards to determine the relevant release date for the order.

Marketing Decision Variables: In any company's marketing program, it is the Marketing Decision Variables that are bound to play a very important role. The best classification of marketing decision variables was given by E. Jerome McCarthy – the "Four P's" – (1) Product (2) Place (3) Promotion and (4) Price.

Marketing Mix: It is the most important task of the Marketing Department to find out the optimum setting for its Marketing Decision Variables. This Optimum Setting is considered the Marketing Mix of the company.

Marketing Effort: Refers to a company's employment of inputs, such as men, material and money, into the company's overall marketing process in order to generate sales.

Marketing Allocation: It refers to a company's allocation of total marketing efforts to its various products, different customer segments, different salesmen and different sales divisions.

Marketing Strategy: It refers to a company's overall objectives, tactics, policies and guidelines that govern over a period of that company's marketing effort.

The strategy spells out the total allocation, the ideal mix required and the level of marketing efforts needed to achieve a predetermined target. Environmental changes and the level of competitive thrust determine the overall strategy.

Consumer Market and an Analysis of Buyer Behavior

Today all markets are complex and unique. To understand the essentials of markets, a marketing system needs a general framework, which tries to understand the market's composition, character, needs and wants. There are four questions that will give an insight into this system.

1. What did the market use to buy? This gives you an insight into the <u>objects</u> of purchase.
2. Why buy? This gives an insight into the <u>objectives</u> of such purchases.
3. Who is buying? This gives an insight into the <u>organization</u> for such purchases.
4. How does it buy? This gives an insight into the general <u>working of the organization</u> that effects purchasing.

THE 4 – P'S OR THE COMPONENTS OF MARKETING DECISION VARIABLES

According to the specific characteristics of individual markets, the 4-P's of Marketing Decision variables are set. In a market where price is most sensitive, the organization tries to maintain the existing price levels even if a price increase from the organization's point of view is justified; it may offer more liberal credit terms or allow some allowances on the basis of more off-take, etc.

Consumer Markets: It is a market where product and services are purchased or hired solely for non-business (personal) consumption. The purchases are made by individuals or households. In the USA consumer markets are huge catering to more than 300 million individuals and families who consume products and services worth many trillions of US Dollars. Marketing people have recognized the existence of different groups and sub-groups within a given market and have developed strategies to cater to each group by developing products and services most suited to their varying needs. They segregate sub groups like: (1) Men, (2) Women, (3) Children, (4) Youth, and (5) Elderly – and offer differentiated products to suit the individual consumer of each such sub group.

Having said that, it is better now for us to postulate a basis for the classification or grouping of a huge number of consumer products so we can get an insight into underlying marketing differences and implications on the Marketing Mix front.

DURABLE GOODS – NON-DURABLE GOODS AND SERVICES

Durable Goods: These tangible goods (actual goods), once bought, will satisfy you for many years (example: air conditioners, refrigerators, clothing, etc.).

Non-Durable Goods: These are also tangible goods, which once bought may be consumed in a very short period of time (example: toothpaste, soap, ham, biscuits, etc.).

Services: These are non-tangible activities, benefits and satisfactions that are offered by individuals with expertise (example: tailoring, hair dressing, cleaning, general repairing, etc.).

The general characteristics in relation to marketing of durable, non-durable and services are:

Durable goods – Needs more personal selling, more seller guarantees and to charge a higher margin.

Non-durable goods and services – To develop loyalty over time, marketed in a number of locations, charging a small margin. Any marketing strategy should be tailored to meet these general characteristics.

Another classification based on consumer's purchasing habits gives us 3 different groups of goods:

(1) Convenient Goods: Goods bought by consumers most often with relative speed without spending time on comparison (Example: Newspapers, soaps, detergents, tobacco products, etc.).

(2) Shopping Goods: Goods bought by consumers after spending time considering its utility, value, quality, suitability, style and of course, price (Example: Cars, home appliances, dress materials, furniture, etc.).

(3) Specialty Goods: Goods bought by consumers that have characteristics perceived to be unique and/or having good brand identification (Example: Branded goods, fancy goods, electronic goods, photographic equipment, etc.).

CONSUMER BEHAVIOR

What are the objectives or goals a consumer while effecting a purchase is looking for? To put it simply, he is looking for a perceived need satisfaction. Needs are unlimited.

Maslow's Hierarchy of Needs

Maslow's Hierarchy of Needs consists of the following stages from the top down:

- Self Actualization
- Esteem Needs
- Belonging and Love
- Safety
- Physical Needs

These stages begin at the physical needs. First you need to have food, water, and shelter before you can worry about other requirements. Once those needs are met you may start to think of other necessities, such as safety. You might buy a gun or move to a more prosperous and safe area. Once you are fed, clothed and safe you will want to meet needs of belonging and love through relationships. If you feel loved, you may begin to think about your self-esteem and how you feel as a person, what you are contributing. The final stage, self-actualization, you may never meet. Most people do not.

Maslow's Hierarchy of Needs

A Buyer's buying decisions are generally influenced by the Buyer's cultural, social, personal and psychological factors. We will presently see all those factors that influence Buyer behavior.

Factors Influencing Buyer Behavior

INTERNATIONAL BUSINESS

Gross National Product is a sum of a country's goods and services produced anywhere in the world. For example, a company in China can have manufacturing plants in the U.S. and in Mexico. The goods produced at those locations would still be included in the GNP.

Gross Domestic Product or GDP is the sum of all final goods and services produced in a country. This would include an Italian company that manufactures something in another country.

Four Asian countries are referred to as the Four Tigers. These countries include Taiwan, Honk Kong, Singapore and South Korea.

Patents are a way to legally protect your idea by preventing other companies from copying your invention. A patent expires after 17 years.

SPECIFIC CASE STUDIES

Joe Camel is the cartoon character created by R. J. Reynolds Tobacco Company to appeal and market to underage buyers. He is as much or more recognizable to children as Mickey Mouse.

Energizer battery has commercials and ad campaigns designed around a drum-banging pink bunny.

FINANCIAL MANAGEMENT

A CPA is an acronym for a Certified Public Accountant. A bull market is when stock prices on average are rising. Junk Bonds are bonds that are rated below Mood's and Standard and Poor's rating or AAA or AA.

Sample Test Questions

1) Which of the following is NOT a part of planning?

    A) Setting goals
    B) Setting objectives
    C) Identifying ways to complete objectives
    D) Conducting meetings
    E) Creating departmental goals

The correct answer is D:) Conducting meeting. While conducting meetings is a part of a manager's role, it is not an official role under the planning category which consists of making departmental goals and objectives and determining how those objectives will be accomplished.

2) PERT is an acronym for what?

    A) Personal effort retention training
    B) Practical employment risk training
    C) Program evaluation and review technique
    D) Personnel employment round table
    E) None of the above

The correct answer is C:) Program evaluation and review technique.

3) Which of the following is NOT a part of a PERT chart?

    A) Optimistic time
    B) Pessimistic time
    C) Time expected
    D) Most probable time
    E) None of the above

The correct answer is E:) None of the above. A PERT chart includes a most pessimistic time, a most optimistic time, time expected, and a most probable time.

4) What theory states "organizational change is inevitable and that organizations and people within the organizations have no other choice except following natural law"?

    A) The Mechanistic Theory
    B) Hierarchy of Needs Theory
    C) The Systems Theory
    D) Hawthorne Effect Theory
    E) None of the above

The correct answer is A:) The Mechanistic Theory.

5) Which of the following theories argues that the effect of studying something/ someone changes the effects of the study?

    A) The Mechanistic Theory
    B) Hierarchy of Needs Theory
    C) The Systems Theory
    D) Hawthorne Effect Theory
    E) None of the above

The correct answer is D:) Hawthorne Effect Theory. This is when the interest in the people's problems affects the outcome, not the changes themselves.

6) Which of the following theories determines interdependence of variables?

    A) The Mechanistic Theory
    B) Hierarchy of Needs Theory
    C) The Systems Theory
    D) Hawthorne Effect Theory
    E) None of the above

The correct answer is C:) The Systems Theory. The Systems Theory deals with inter-dependence instead of independence of variables and their interactions. It started with a more intensive, very broad, wide-angle – involving a number of variables to measure complex inter-relationships – and inclusive viewpoint. Group behavior is seen in the system as broadly shaped and influenced.

7) Which is the second stage of Maslow's Hierarchy of Needs?

   A) Self-actualization
   B) Esteem needs
   C) Belonging and love
   D) Safety
   E) Physical needs

The correct answer is D:) Safety. Safety is the second stage in Maslow's Hierarchy of Needs.

8) When something is measurable in number it is

   A) Naturalistic observation
   B) Qualitative
   C) Cross sectional studies
   D) Quantitative
   E) Extinction

The correct answer is D:) Quantitative. When something can be measured with numbers, like a completed number of surveys, it is considered quantitative.

9) Who is considered to be the father of modern management?

   A) Abraham Maslow
   B) Max Weber
   C) Chester Barnard
   D) Frederick Herzberg
   E) Peter Drucker

The correct answer is E:) Peter Drucker. Peter Drucker is considered the father of Modern Management.

10) Who completed a study on the fastest and most efficient way to do a job?

   A) Frank Gilbreth
   B) Peter Drucker
   C) Max Weber
   D) Henry Gantt
   E) None of the above

The correct answer is A:) Frank Gilbreth. Frank and Lillian Gilbreth did a study on the most efficient way to do a job.

11) _____ is a way to show the time needed to complete a long or complicated project.

    A) PERT
    B) Critical Path Method
    C) Bar Chart
    D) Gantt Chart
    E) Pie Chart

The correct answer is D:) Gantt chart. A Gantt chart is used to show who will be working on or different stages of a project and the time each step takes.

12) Which person created the five management functions?

    A) Frank Gilbreth
    B) Peter Drucker
    C) Henry Fayol
    D) Max Weber
    E) Henry Gantt

The correct answer is C:) Henry Fayol. Henry Fayol is credited with creating the five management functions which are (1) planning, (2) organizing, (3) commanding, (4) coordinating, and (5) controlling.

13) LPC stands for

    A) Least personnel count
    B) Leverage people credentials
    C) Late potential credit
    D) Least preferred coworker
    E) None of the above

The correct answer is D:) Least preferred coworker. The LPC or least preferred coworker is an important part of Fiedler's contingency theory.

14) Which of the following are the levels of management?

    A) Technical, interpersonal and conceptual
    B) Technical, interpersonal and line staff
    C) Training, managing, staffing
    D) Controlling, planning, retaining
    E) None of the above

The correct answer is A:) Technical, interpersonal and conceptual.

15) Your company participates in an Affirmative Action program. As a manager you interview two equally individuals for a new position. One candidate is white and one candidate is a pacific islander. What do you do?

    A) Hire the white candidate
    B) Hire the pacific islander candidate
    C) Hire neither and conduct more interviews
    D) Hire towards the quota determined by your HR department
    E) Consult with in house counsel and let them make the decision

The correct answer is D:) Hire towards the quota determined by your HR department. Affirmative Action programs are custom created for each organization in a certain geographic area. Affirmative Action gives minorities, including women, additional opportunities in the workforce.

16) Which of the following is considered a pioneer in management theory?

    A) Peter Drucker
    B) Mary Parker Follet
    C) Frank Gilbreth
    D) Henry Fayol
    E) Frederick Herzberg

The correct answer is B:) Mary Parker Follet. This woman from the late 1800s wrote many books on management theory, and human relations. She also worked as a speaker and volunteer social worker.

17) Which of the following terms illustrates the order of authority in an organization?

    A) Flow chart
    B) PERT chart
    C) Chain of command
    D) Town hall
    E) None of the above

The correct answer is C:) Chain of command. The chain of command is a term that refers to who reports to who in an organization. An organizational chart would show this as well.

18) In Herzberg's Motivation-Hygiene theory, the Hygiene refers to what?

    A) Cleanliness
    B) Work environment
    C) Satisfiers
    D) Motivators
    E) Dissatisfiers

The correct answer is E:) Dissatisfiers. Herzberg's Motivation-Hygiene theory basically found what makes an employee satisfied. He called something that was a motivation a satisfier and anything that was a dissatisfier was referred to as hygiene.

19) When you find the answer to your problem but settle for something else is an example of the

    A) Implicit favorite model
    B) Bounded rationality model
    C) Econological model
    D) Morality model
    E) Ethical model

The correct answer is B:) Bounded rationality model.

20) When you choose the solution that has the greatest benefit for you

    A) Implicit favorite model
    B) Bounded rationality model
    C) Econological model
    D) Morality model
    E) Ethical model

The correct answer is C:) Econological model.

21) Which of the following people was associated with the Hawthorne Effect study?

    A) Peter Drucker
    B) Mary Parker Follet
    C) Elton Mayo
    D) Frank Gilbreth
    E) James Smith

The correct answer is C:) Elton Mayo. Elton Mayo is also considered the founder of the Human Relations Movement.

22) If you are an authoritarian, you ascribe to

A) Theory X
B) Theory Y
C) Theory XY
D) Management theory
E) None of the above

The correct answer is A:) Theory X.

23) Which of the following is considered the father of strategic planning?

A) Peter Drucker
B) Chester Barnard
C) Elton Mayo
D) Frank Gilbreth
E) James Smith

The correct answer is B:) Chester Barnard. Chester Barnard is considered the father of strategic planning.

24) Which of the following developed the acceptance theory?

A) Peter Drucker
B) Chester Barnard
C) Elton Mayo
D) Frank Gilbreth
E) James Smith

The correct answer is B:) Chester Barnard. Chester Barnard felt that the authority did not reside on the person giving the orders, but in the minds and will of the subordinates that determined whether to accept or reject those order from above. If these four areas were met then the employee accepted the task or authority: 1) the employee must understand what is asked of them. 2) they agree that the task is in congruence with the goals of the organization. 3) they agreed that the task was in their own personal interest. 4) they were physically and mentally able to comply.

25) A manager who believes that all people are valuable and want to contribute to their best ability you ascribe to

    A) Theory X
    B) Theory Y
    C) Theory XY
    D) Management theory
    E) None of the above

The correct answer is B:) Theory Y.

26) Which of the following is NOT a contributor to an employee's attitude?

    A) Previous jobs
    B) Education
    C) Peers
    D) Family
    E) None of the above

The correct answer is B:) Education. Education is generally not considered a contributor to an employee's attitude.

27) When someone is producing at standard it is called

    A) Role
    B) Role conflict
    C) Norm
    D) Status
    E) None of the above

The correct answer is C:) Norm. A norm or status quo is considered standard.

28) Who created the contingency theory?

    A) Peter Drucker
    B) Chester Barnard
    C) Elton Mayo
    D) Frank Gilbreth
    E) Fred Fiedler

The correct answer is E:) Fred Fiedler. Fred Fiedler created the contingency theory.

29) What standard is the following "Giving monetary values to realized sales"?

    A) Physical standard
    B) Capital standard
    C) Revenue standard
    D) Cost standard
    E) Intangible standard

The correct answer is C:) Revenue standard.

30) What standard is the following "monetary value for the cost of operations, such as machine-hour-costs, cost of material per unit, cost of labor per unit, cost per unit of sales, etc."?

    A) Physical standard
    B) Capital standard
    C) Revenue standard
    D) Cost standard
    E) Intangible standard

The correct answer is D:) Cost standard.

31) What standard is the following "quantified standards at the operating level. Products produced in numbers, in value, material used in weightage and value, labor employed in house and in value, services rendered in value, etc."?

    A) Physical standard
    B) Capital standard
    C) Revenue standard
    D) Cost standard
    E) Intangible standard

The correct answer is A:) Physical standard.

32) Which of the following is NOT one of Henry Mintzberg's classifications of organizations?

A) Simple
B) Complex
C) Organic
D) Stable
E) Dynamic

The correct answer is C:) Organic. Henry Mintzberg classified organizations as either simple, complex, stable or dynamic.

33) A good TQM program does NOT include

A) Determination of standards of quality
B) Institution of an effective continuous on the job checking program with responsibilities and accountability firmly fixed
C) A recording system for comparing errors vs. standards
D) A method which alternatives to solutions
E) To install a program of analysis and quality improvement whenever found needed

The correct answer is D:) A method which alternatives to solutions. A good TQM is made up of: (1) determination of standards of quality, (2) institution of an effective continuous on the job checking program with responsibilities and accountability firmly fixed, (3) a recording system for comparing errors vs. standards, (4) a method which spells out corrective action, and (5) to install a program of analysis and quality improvement whenever found needed.

34) Which of the following is NOT a protected Title VII class?

A) Race
B) Age
C) Sexual preference
D) Religion
E) None of the above

The correct answer is C:) Sexual preference.

35) Which of the following is NOT an example of traditional authority?

      A) Supervisor
      B) Vice President
      C) Bishop
      D) Secretary
      E) Father

The correct answer is D:) Secretary.

36) Which of the following is responsible for ensuring employee safety?

      A) OSHA
      B) EEO
      C) Department of Labor
      D) COBRA
      E) FBLA

The correct answer is A:) OSHA.

37) Which of the following is NOT a way to deal with risk?

      A) Assuming
      B) Avoiding
      C) Shifting
      D) Deflecting
      E) Calculating

The correct answer is D:) Deflecting.

38) Which of the following is an example of environmental stress?

      A) Construction noise
      B) Strong perfume
      C) Peers
      D) Broken heating unit
      E) None of the above

The correct answer is A:) Construction noise.

39) Which of the following is an example of Maslow's first level of needs?

  A) Food
  B) Car
  C) School
  D) Church
  E) None of the above

The correct answer is A:) Food.

40) Which is the second stage of Maslow's Hierarchy of Needs?

  A) Self-actualization
  B) Esteem needs
  C) Safety needs
  D) Physical needs
  E) Belonging needs

The correct answer is C:) Safety needs.

41) When you choose the best action for each situation

  A) Situational leadership
  B) Participative leadership
  C) Autocratic leadership
  D) Laissez faire leadership
  E) None of the above

The correct answer is A:) Situational leadership.

42) When a supervisor asks for opinions in making decisions

  A) Situational leadership
  B) Participative leadership
  C) Autocratic leadership
  D) Laissez faire leadership
  E) None of the above

The correct answer is B:) Participative leadership.

43) Which of the following is a union function?

    A) Negotiate pay
    B) Creating new business policies
    C) Budgeting
    D) Creating statistical reports
    E) None of the above

The correct answer is A:) Negotiate pay.

44) Which of the following is an example of Maslow's third level of needs?

    A) Sex
    B) Money
    C) Love
    D) Home
    E) Shoes

The correct answer is C:) Love.

45) Which of the following is NOT part of a training program?

    A) Job sharing
    B) Job rotating
    C) Temporary promotion
    D) Promotion
    E) None of the above

The correct answer is D:) Promotion.

46) Which of the following is an industry commonly known to have line employees?

    A) Automotive
    B) Woodworking
    C) Education
    D) Retail
    E) Hospitality

The correct answer is A:) Automotive.

47) Hands off leadership is also called

    A) Situational leadership
    B) Participative leadership
    C) Autocratic leadership
    D) Laissez faire leadership
    E) None of the above

The correct answer is D:) Laissez faire leadership.

48) Which of the following tells employees and others what is the main purpose of the company is

    A) Vision
    B) Mission statement
    C) Company statement
    D) Business plan
    E) None of the above

The correct answer is B:) Mission statement.

49) A policy can be defined as a _____ action course that serves as a guide for the identified and accepted objectives and goals.

    A) Predefined
    B) Flexible
    C) Necessary
    D) Unknown
    E) None of the above

The correct answer is A:) Predefined.

50) A totalitarian leader

    A) Situational leadership
    B) Participative leadership
    C) Autocratic leadership
    D) Laissez faire leadership
    E) None of the above

The correct answer is C:) Autocratic leadership.

51) The way that people communicate with each other using their bodies

    A) Consideration
    B) Body language
    C) Communication
    D) Charisma
    E) None of the above

The correct answer is B:) Body language.

52) Leadership characteristics that inspire employees is called

    A) Chain of command
    B) Vision
    C) Charisma
    D) Motivation
    E) None of the above

The correct answer is C:) Charisma.

53) Agreement of members of a group on a decision is called

    A) Consensus
    B) Group think
    C) Meetings
    D) Consideration
    E) None of the above

The correct answer is A:) Consensus.

54) Leaders that use group ideas to make decisions

    A) Autocratic
    B) Laissez-faire
    C) Democratic
    D) Trait
    E) None of the above

The correct answer is D:) Trait.

55) Which is NOT a factor that influences the favorableness of a leader?

    A) Leader-member relations
    B) Task structure
    C) Leader position power
    D) Charisma level
    E) None of the above

The correct answer is D:) Charisma level.

56) A billboard is an example of

    A) Active listening
    B) Two-way communication
    C) One-way communication
    D) None of the above
    E) None of the above

The correct answer is C:) One-way communication.

57) Leaders that give the group total freedom

    A) Autocratic
    B) Laissez-faire
    C) Democratic
    D) Trait
    E) None of the above

The correct answer is B:) Laissez-faire. 54 Principles of Management.

58) Which of the following is NOT a communication pattern?

    A) Chain
    B) Circle
    C) Wheel
    D) Arc
    E) None of the above

The correct answer is D:) Arc.

59) When someone receives too much information and cannot tell what is important from what is not it is called

   A) Overload
   B) Spam
   C) Decoding information
   D) Rejected information
   E) None of the above

The correct answer is A:) Overload.

60) When someone deliberately tampers with a message, leaving out information, it is called

   A) Overload
   B) Omitting
   C) Y pattern
   D) Highlighting
   E) None of the above

The correct answer is B:) Omitting.

61) Which of the following is NOT a supervisory function?

   A) Marketing
   B) Planning
   C) Staffing
   D) Organizing
   E) None of the above

The correct answer is A:) Marketing.

62) Which of the following is an example of an extrinsic reward?

   A) Raise
   B) Self-esteem
   C) Praise
   D) Personal development
   E) None of the above

The correct answer is A:) Raise.

63) If a plant manager is tasked to reduce costs by 10% this is an example of what kind of goal?

    A) Strategic
    B) Long-term
    C) Tactical
    D) Operational
    E) Realistic

The correct answer is D:) Operational.

64) Which of the following shows the relationship between employees and their peers?

    A) Organizational chart
    B) Gantt chart
    C) Decision tree
    D) Simulation
    E) PERT chart

The correct answer is A:) Organizational chart.

65) Which of the following shows alternate paths for decision making?

    A) Organizational chart
    B) Gantt chart
    C) Decision tree
    D) Simulation
    E) None of the above

The correct answer is C:) Decision tree.

66) When a supervisor administers a questionnaire among participants that have never met it is called

    A) Brainstorming
    B) Sampling
    C) Delphi technique
    D) Groupthink
    E) Questionnaire

The correct answer is D:) Delphi technique.

67) Which of the following shows timelines for projects?

    A) Organizational chart
    B) Gantt chart
    C) Decision tree
    D) Simulation
    E) None of the above

The correct answer is B:) Gantt chart.

68) Who created Theory X and Theory Y?

    A) Max Weber
    B) Abraham Maslow
    C) Douglas McGregor
    D) Frank Gilbreth
    E) Henry Fayol

The correct answer is C:) Douglas McGregor.

69) When two groups or individuals work together to resolve a problem it is called

    A) Negotiation
    B) Grievance
    C) Arbitration
    D) Mediation
    E) None of the above

The correct answer is A:) Negotiation.

70) What is it called when a third party is facilitating negotiations?

    A) Concession
    B) Grievance
    C) Arbitration
    D) Mediation
    E) None of the above

The correct answer is D:) Mediation.

71) An employee that works on an assembly line performing the same task again and again is an example of

    A) Job specialization
    B) Job rotation
    C) Job sharing
    D) Job description
    E) Job requirement

The correct answer is A:) Job specialization.

72) Two receptionists work at Widget, Inc., one in the morning and one in the afternoon. They are an example of

    A) Job specialization
    B) Job rotation
    C) Job sharing
    D) Job control
    E) None of the above

The correct answer is C:) Job sharing.

73) When a person acts as expected as part of the group they are portraying their

    A) Role
    B) Groupthink
    C) Norm
    D) Status rank
    E) Mole

The correct answer is A:) Role.

74) Who first studied job motions with bricklayers, studying how fewer hand motions made the work faster?

    A) Max Weber
    B) Abraham Maslow
    C) Douglas McGregor
    D) Frank Gilbreth
    E) Fredrick Hertzberg

The correct answer is D:) Frank Gilbreth.

75) What is it called when a third party of empowered to resolve a disagreement it is called?

    A) Negotiation
    B) Grievance
    C) Arbitration
    D) Mediation
    E) None of the above

The correct answer is C:) Arbitration.

76) Who was a proponent of bureaucracy?

    A) Max Weber
    B) Abraham Maslow
    C) Douglas McGregor
    D) Frank Gilbreth
    E) Fredrick Hertzberg

The correct answer is A:) Max Weber.

77) Which of the following can NOT be discussed in a job interview?

    A) Education and degrees
    B) Children
    C) Previous wages
    D) Personality
    E) Salary

The correct answer is B:) Children.

78) The grapevine of the organization is everything BUT

    A) Formal
    B) Generally accurate
    C) Verbal
    D) Exists in every organization
    E) None of the above

The correct answer is A:) Formal.

79) When a supervisor believes that all employees like work it is called

   A) Theory Y
   B) Theory X
   C) Hawthorne Effect
   D) TQM
   E) Humanistic Theory

The correct answer is A:) Theory Y.

80) This scientific study originally tested worker's output and light, later revealing unintended consequences

   A) Theory Y
   B) Theory X
   C) Hawthorne Effect
   D) TQM
   E) Contingency Theory

The correct answer is C:) Hawthorne Effect.

81) Referent power is the same as

   A) Lassaize faire leadership
   B) Charismatic leadership
   C) Peer pressure
   D) Expert leadership
   E) None of the above

The correct answer is B:) Charismatic leadership.

82) Legitimate power is the same as

   A) Lassaize faire leadership
   B) Traditional leadership
   C) Peer pressure
   D) Expert leadership
   E) None of the above

The correct answer is B:) Traditional leadership.

83) Regarding sexual harassment which of the following is NOT true

    A) Offenders can be same or opposite sex
    B) Victims do not have to be harassed personally but affected through environment
    C) Harasser must be a superior employee
    D) Harassment may occur without economic injury
    E) None of the above

The correct answer is C:) Harasser must be a superior employee.

84) Who created a system of human needs and motivations?

    A) Max Weber
    B) Abraham Maslow
    C) Douglas McGregor
    D) Frank Gilbreth
    E) Peter Drucker

The correct answer is B:) Abraham Maslow.

85) Long term success through customer satisfaction

    A) Theory Y
    B) Theory X
    C) Hawthorne Effect
    D) TQM
    E) Contingency Theory

The correct answer is D:) TQM.

86) Who was responsible for developing the 14 principles of management?

    A) Max Weber
    B) Henri Fayol
    C) Douglas McGregor
    D) Frank Gilbreth
    E) Peter Drucker

The correct answer is B:) Henry Fayol.

87) Which of the following are barriers to making decisions?

    A) Statistics
    B) Lack of statistics
    C) Emotions
    D) All of the above
    E) None of the above

The correct answer is D:) All of the above.

88) Which of the following is NOT a type of resistance?

    A) Logical
    B) Psychological
    C) Sociological
    D) Biological
    E) All of the above

The correct answer is D:) Biological.

89) The organizational structure where organizations are divided by products or divisions

    A) Functional
    B) Line and staff
    C) Product
    D) Matrix
    E) None of the above

The correct answer is C:) Product.

90) Who believed that managers make decisions based on their assumptions of human nature?

    A) McGregor
    B) Taylor
    C) Ratter
    D) Johnson
    E) Maslow

The correct answer is A:) McGregor.

91) When an interest in the people's problems affects the outcome, not the changes themselves, it is known as

    A) Hawthorne effect
    B) Taylor effect
    C) Laissez faire effect
    D) Groupthink effect
    E) Hygiene theory

The correct answer is A:) Hawthorne effect.

92) Factor that always stays the same

    A) Dependent variable
    B) Independent variable
    C) Constant
    D) Correlation
    E) Statistic

The correct answer is C:) Constant.

93) Information that is difficult to measure is called

    A) Quantitative
    B) Qualitative
    C) Longitudinal
    D) Dependent
    E) Constant

The correct answer is B:) Qualitative.

94) If you believe that all people are good – you ascribe to this school of thought

    A) Biological
    B) Cognitive
    C) Structuralism
    D) Humanistic
    E) Cultural

The correct answer is D:) Humanistic.

95) Standards or principles

    A) Norms
    B) Values
    C) Rules
    D) Status quo
    E) Groups

The correct answer is B:) Values.

96) Which of the following is NOT a factor with job satisfaction?

    A) Hours
    B) Pay
    C) Benefits
    D) Vacation location
    E) Working conditions

The correct answer is D:) Vacation location.

97) When a person responds to a neutral stimulus _____ is being used.

    A) Classical conditioning
    B) Operant conditioning
    C) Extrinsic reinforcer
    D) Intrinsic reinforcer
    E) None of the above

The correct answer is A:) Classical conditioning.

98) Clayton Alderfer created his ERG theory based on the work of which theorist?

    A) Max Weber
    B) Henri Fayol
    C) Abraham Maslow
    D) Frank Gilbreth
    E) Peter Drucker

The correct answer is C;) Abraham Maslow. Alderfer wanted to revise Maslow's Hierarchy of Needs to match empirical research.

99) When you are a secretary and there are seven levels between your role and the CEO, your organization is considered to be

A) Fat
B) Tall
C) Flat
D) Short
E) Huge

The correct answer is B:) Tall. A tall organization is one when the organizational chart is drawn out is tall.

100) A flat organization is an organization with

A) A high ratio of mid level management to high level management positions.
B) A low ratio of mid level management to low level employee positions.
C) A low number (if any) of mid level management positions.
D) A high ratio of low level employees to potential customers.
E) None of the above

The correct answer is C:) A low number (if any) of mid level management positions. This way the top level management comes into direct contact with the low level employees.

Test Taking Strategies

Here are some test-taking strategies that are specific to this test and to other DSST tests in general:

- Keep your eyes on the time. Pay attention to how much time you have left.

- Read the entire question and read all the answers. Many questions are not as hard to answer as they may seem. Sometimes, a difficult sounding question really only is asking you how to read an accompanying chart. Chart and graph questions are on most DANTES/DSST tests and should be an easy free point.

- If you don't know the answer immediately, the new computer-based testing lets you mark questions and come back to them later if you have time.

- Read the wording carefully. Some words can give you hints to the right answer. There are no exceptions to an answer when there are words in the question such as always, all or none. If one of the answer choices includes most or some of the right answers, but not all, then that is not the answer. Here is an example:

> The primary colors include all of the following:
> A) Red, Yellow, Blue, Green
> B) Red, Green, Yellow
> C) Red, Orange, Yellow
> D) Red, Yellow, Blue

Although item A includes all the right answers, it also includes an incorrect answer, making it incorrect. If you didn't read it carefully, were in a hurry, or didn't know the material well, you might fall for this.

- Make a guess on a question that you do not know the answer to. There is no penalty for an incorrect answer. Eliminate the answer choices that you know are incorrect. For example, this will let your guess be a 1 in 3 chance instead.

What Your Score Means

Based on your score, you may, or may not, qualify for credit at your specific institution. The current ACE recommended score for this exam is 46. Your school may require a higher or lower score to receive credit. To find out what score you need for credit, you need to get that information from your school's website or academic advisor.

You lose no points for incorrect questions so make sure you answer each question. If you don't know, make an educated guess. On this particular test, you must answer 100 questions in 90 minutes.

Test Preparation

How much you need to study depends on your knowledge of a subject area. If you are interested in literature, took it in school, or enjoy reading then your study and preparation for the literature or humanities test will not need to be as intensive as that of someone who is new to literature.

This book is much different than the regular CLEP study guides. This book actually teaches you the information that you need to know to pass the test. If you are particularly interested in an area, or feel that you want more information, do a quick search online. We've tried not to include too much depth in areas that are not as essential on the test. It is important to understand all major theories and concepts listed in the table of contents. It is also important to know any bolded words.

Don't worry if you do not understand or know a lot about the area. With minimal study, you can complete and pass the test.

One of the fallacies of other test books is test questions. People assume that the content of the questions are similar to what will be on the test. That is not the case. They are only there to test your "test taking skills" so for those who know to read a question carefully, there is not much added value from taking a "fake" test. So we have constructed our test questions differently. We will use them to teach you new information not covered in the study guide AND to test your knowledge of items you should already know from reading the text. If you don't know the answer to the test question, review the material. If it is new information, then this is an area that will be covered on the test but not in detail.

To prepare for the test, make a series of goals. Allot a certain amount of time to review the information you have already studied and to learn additional material. Take notes as you study; it will help you learn the material. If you haven't done so already, download the study tips guide from the website and use it to start your study plan.

✒ *Legal Note*

FLASHCARDS

This section contains flashcards for you to use to further your understanding of the material and test yourself on important concepts, names or dates. You can cut these out to study from or keep them in the study guide, flipping the page over to check yourself.

Management Theory: Empirical/Case Approach

Management Theory: Interpersonal Behavior Approach

Management Theory: Group Behavior Approach

Management Theory: Cooperative Social Systems Approach

Management Theory: Sociotechnical Systems Approach

Management Theory: Decision Theory Approach

Management Theory: Systems Approach

Management Theory: Mathematical or Management Science Approach

Understanding people and relationships. If people were understood perfectly, reaching organizational goals would not be difficult

The experience of past situations guide the present. Find out why an action succeeded or failed by analyzing the basic reasons

Propounded by Christian Barnard, it is the cooperative interaction of thoughts, ideas, wants and desires of two or more people

Work in groups rather than in isolation. The study of how behavior patterns in groups affect production

A manager's most important function is decision making and therefore decisions should be the central focus. All other functions of a manager are built around decisions

Credited to E.L. Trist, this approach seeks to emphasize the systems aspect of group behavior

Mathematical models forms part of this theory. Each situation is fraught in terms of available mathematical models and then analyzes the situation threadbare arriving at a mathematically correct decision

Management is a system, which envelops within itself many subsystems, all operating within the total environment

Management Theory: Contingency or Situational Approach

Management Theory: Managerial Roles Approach

Management Theory: Operational Approach

Economic Environment

Technological Environment

Social Environment

Political and Legal Environment

Ethical Environment

Propounded by Professor Henry Mintzberg. Observing what other mangers do, then using such observations as a platform for analyzing and concluding on the basis of such analysis

Any manager's performance is directly related to a set of given circumstance or contingency. Some theorist also feel that it takes into account not only situations but also on the behavior

Availability of capital, rate of interest, labor availability and how well things are organized, general price levels, the degree of productivity, the willingness of entrepreneurs and availability of managerial skills

Imparting knowledge from every other field of knowledge such as sociology, mathematics, economics, psychology etc.

Value systems unique to particular group of people or society. The value system consists of attitudes, behavior patterns, needs, wants, expectations, level of education, the degree of intelligence, general beliefs, customs and traditions

How good the available knowledge is used through technology is a factor to reckon with. How to conceive ideas, how to design, how to produce optimally, how to effect efficient distribution and how well marketing is done, are technology oriented

Holding on to moral principles of what is right and what is wrong, guided by value systems prevalent in society and generally behaving in a responsible way

Laws, rules, regulations, governmental polices that affect an organization

Social Responsibilities

Steps in Planning

Mechanistic Theory

Systems Theory

Revenue Standards

Frederick Taylor

PERT stands for what?

Self-actualization

Analysis of opportunities. Setting of objectives. Identify the basis. Compare alternatives. Design relevant plans. Quantify for control.

Organizations as well as mangers should be socially responsive to the society as a whole and should be able to do their bit when a situation calls for it

Organizational processes should be guided and influenced because all things are interdependent

Organizational change is inevitable and natural processes should be allowed to take their own course

Scientific management school

Giving monetary value to realized sales

Highest need in Maslow's hierarchy - Level 5

Program evaluation and review technique

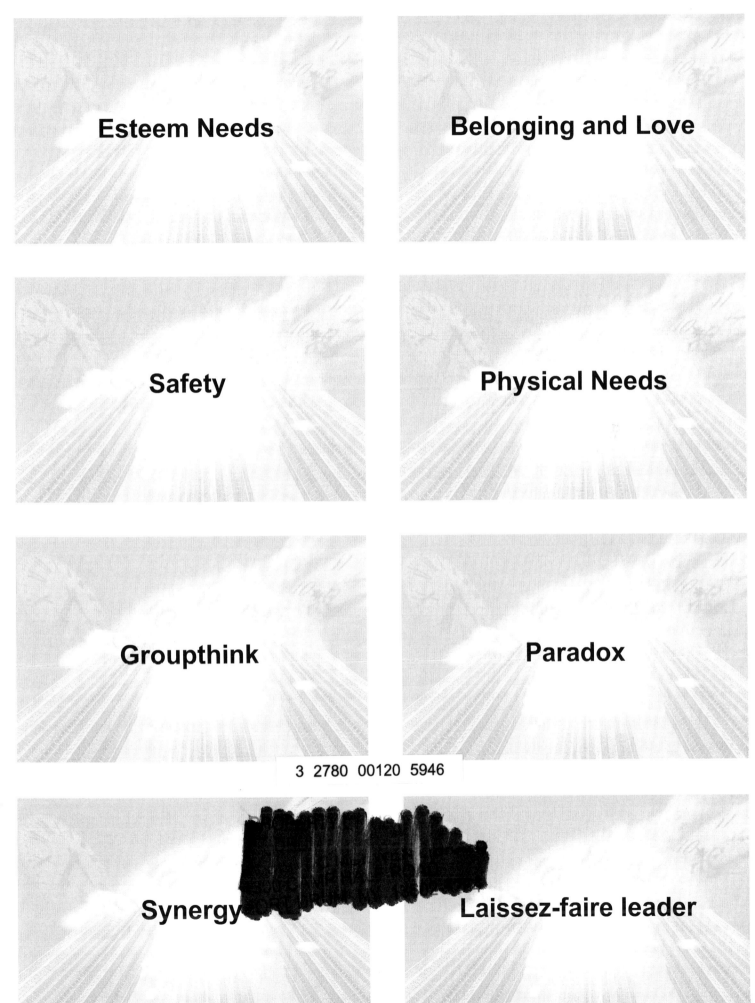

Esteem Needs

Belonging and Love

Safety

Physical Needs

Groupthink

Paradox

3 2780 00120 5946

Synergy

Laissez-faire leader

Level 3 need

Level 4 need

Level 1 need

Level 2 need

Contradictory Conclusion

Conformity in a group
situation

Hands off leadership

Cooperative action